Hard Core Poor

A book about making your money stretch like a yoga master!

Table of Contents

Pg 7 - Introduction -What is "poor"? And more importantly, what is "Hard Core Poor"?

Pg 13 - Do you want to be debt-free?

Pg 17 - I'm a fan of Dave.

Pg 23 - So, now what?

Pg 25 - Clutter busting

Pg 33 - Housing

Pg 49 - Heating and Cooling

Pg 67 – Electricity

Pg 73 – Transportation

Pg 87 - Food

Pg 97 – Clothing

Pg 105 - Laundry

Pg 113 - Cleaning Supplies

Pg 117 – Beauty and Hygeine

Pg 127 - Technology

Pg 133 – Entertainment

Pg 139 – Phone

Pg 143 – Internet

Pg 147 – Banking (or how to access your money when the banks won't work with you)

Pg 156– Taxes

Pg 160 – KIDS –

    Baby Needs

    Food

    Car Seats

    Clothing

    Cribs

    Diapers

    Assorted Baby Gear

Pg 192 - School

Pg 199 - College

Pg 209 - Increasing Income

Pg 219 - When You're Out Of The Woods

What is "poor"? And more importantly, what is "Hard Core Poor"?

"Poor" has a rather loose definition lately. "Poor" people in our country can drive cars, have household appliances, TVs, and various other "valuable" goods. But what many people from the outside don't see is that the car is an $800 beater that needs $2000 worth of work, you found the TV on the side of the road (and it works fine) and the fancy bread maker cost $3 at the thrift store. So let's just define poor as a lack of available cash to pay the bills, buy food, and pay for transportation.

"Hard Core Poor" is a phrase I developed many years ago when I was flat broke. "Hard Core Poor" is the willingness to do something unusual, old-fashioned, or seemingly desperate (like washing your clothes by hand) in order to save some of that precious cash for the bills or food. It's using your time and creativity instead of paying someone else for their time and creativity. Someone who is Hard Core Poor might cook from scratch, pick a neighbors' leftover fruit from their tree (with permission) and preserve it, learn to sew simple projects for themselves or for gifts or to sell, and learn to maintain and repair their own homes and cars. They might come up with little ways to bring in extra cash now and then, like baking cookies to sell at Christmas, doing laundry for busy neighbors, picking up cans and turning them in at the recycling center, driving people for their errands and appointments to earn gas money, or picking up a few extra dollars online by doing some writing assignments or using a search engine that pays you in cash or rewards.

Hard Core Poor living can seem like a lot of work, and it is. You're replacing the need for money with the work of your hands, or earning more money by working for it. It might seem occasionally unfair, and I agree. **Life isn't fair. Poverty isn't fair. It stinks!** We can stamp our feet and complain, but that doesn't pay the bills or put dinner on the table. Some strategies might work for you, others won't make sense for you to try because it won't save you money or you live in an area where the strategy doesn't apply. The point is to get you thinking – to help you use your God-given creativity to get you through the hard times.

Why did **I** write this book? I mean me, as opposed to anyone else? I'm pretty comfortable these days, but in 2002 I was fired from a reasonably well-paying job when I was 8 months pregnant with my first child. My now-ex brought home a quarter of my previous income. We had been struggling a bit before, lining up bills to eliminate with each check, but now we were desperate. Where using the laundromat was once an inconvenience, now it was an expensive luxury. I took a job as a convenience store clerk 2 blocks from our home (we shuffled schedules so someone was always with the baby), we sold trash-picked items at the flea market a few miles away, and after about a year my mother helped me buy a small consignment store within walking distance, which we ran with the baby on my hip for 2 years before we had to sell it during my second pregnancy. Most of this time we either had either one working car or none at all. Everything had to be planned around bus schedules, bike rides, dropping each other off, getting rides from friends, and what we could carry in stroller baskets.

After my ex and I split up, my parents took in me and my children. I paid them $200 rent every month that I was working, and I can never say enough about all they did to support me. They helped me through the nightmare of day care pickups and drop offs, helped me care for the kids when I was exhausted, and put up with us living there for a lot longer than I ever meant them to. I managed to pay off all the debt accumulated in my name while I was with my ex - $7,000 paid off while on an income of about $13,000 a year (though I did bargain down some of the creditors).

I had hoped to be self supporting for a long time, but due to a combination of work problems, my own health problems, and a health problem of my daughters that prevented her from being in a standard school for a time, I found myself unable to hold a real job. I sold Avon for a while, took on cleaning jobs, and did as many money saving tricks as I knew to avoid having to rely on my parents for too much. (Child support came, but not often and not much.)

I was blessed to meet my husband and the love of my life in that time, and he fell in love with all of us! He was thrifty already, owning his own fixer-upper home and managing his money well. Even so, I had tricks to teach him. We often brag to each other about how little we spend on just about everything. We had another baby in 2013, and while he has had everything he needed, we have been able to spend less than $400 for everything he needed in his first year of life! Money is still – and always – something we have to watch, but now our savings actually get SAVED, instead of being funneled into other needs like gas for the cars.

Why did I write this book? Because I lived in fear of having the power cut off, and the reality of having our phone cut off. Because I made bad decisions when I was broke, and those decisions made me broke-er. Because I learned how to make better decisions as I got better. I wrote this book to the me of 2002, telling her everything I wish I had known then. I hope someone that reads this book going through a 2002 of their own will be able to use these tricks to make their money stretch a little easier.

Do you want to be debt-free?

It's an honest question. For some people, being debt free is so far off it's almost insulting to ask the question. (You can still do it!) For some people, being debt free is a serious goal, but they don't quite know how to get there on their current income. And still other people don't see what the big deal is – as long as you can make your payments, why bother being debt free?

To the third group – most of the people in the first two groups had the same mind frame that you did, but something happened. They may have lost a job, had an unexpected (though welcomed) baby, been right-sized, down-sized, had a pay cut, got a divorce, had an adult kid get married or move back home... you get the idea. LIFE happened, and suddenly those payments weren't as easy to make. People who took great pride in paying off their credit cards at the end of each month started having trouble making more than the minimum payments, and interest started to pile up. Student loans were put into deferment or were even defaulted. Some lost their homes or apartments because they could no longer manage their mortgage or rent payments.

To the people in those first two groups – does all that sound familiar? You may be kicking yourselves, thinking "If I had only...", wishing that you had known what was coming. You might be feeling hopeless, like nothing will EVER be the way it should again. You may feel angry because you enjoyed the life you had, and now you feel insulted and low because you can no longer afford those luxuries you enjoyed. I want you to know that first of all, those feelings are normal. It's OK to feel that way, at least at first. But my hope is that this book will show you not only how to save money, but to ENJOY your life while you pay off those soul-crushing bills.

This is not a finance book, per se – there are many other people far better than I who can counsel you on your actual finances, though I'll give you a few tips. Since you're reading this, I assume that you already want to follow a plan to get out of debt, but you're having trouble finding the "extra" money every month to get those payments going. I will do my best to show you where my friends, family and I have learned to save money, and hopefully you'll be able to use that knowledge to get those debts paid! If your main challenge is just meeting your monthly living expenses (forget about debt, you're trying to survive), hopefully we'll help you there too.

I'm a fan of Dave.

My favorite debt-busting program is Dave Ramsey's – if you aren't in an area where you can listen to him on the radio, I recommend listening to an episode or two on his website, daveramsey.com . It's inspiring to hear the stories of men and women who buckled down, scrimped, saved, and paid off enormous loads of debt in what seems like an unbelievably short amount of time. Since Dave mentions his Baby Steps to financial freedom on his radio program and on his website, I'm sure he won't mind if I re-state them here. Before you even begin, cut up your credit cards and make sure your rent/mortgage, utilities and groceries are paid for – if you're having trouble with even that, hopefully the tips in this book will help you get to a better place.

Step-before-step 1: Get out all your bills, your income statements, your receipts from last month, and figure out how much money you have and where it's going (or should be going). A lot of people drift through life, never paying attention to how much they spend, because it's "just" $10. Every dollar, every dime counts, but it only seems that way when you're working toward a goal. So here are some goals!

Step 1: Save a small emergency fund. Dave defines this as $1000, but if your income is under $25,000 he suggests $500. This is to catch those sudden car repairs, emergency room co-pays, and other "life" moments so you don't fall behind on your current bills to pay for them. $500 when you're broke sounds almost impossible to save – you might have to do it a few dollars at a time – but imagine the security of knowing that the next time the car breaks down, you won't have to go around to all your friends and family for help or ask the garage to let you pay in installments. I know how embarrassing that is, and how it strips you of your dignity. Every dollar you save for those emergencies is a down payment on reclaiming your dignity.

Step 2: Take all your bills except your mortgage (if you have one), line them up, and pay the minimum on all but the smallest. If the total "minimums" add up to more than you have available, contact the companies and negotiate a smaller minimum for the time being. No matter what they tell you (we have to get x amount every month and we can't go below that), if you are making small, good faith payments on your debt, they will work with you. The collectors are being pressured to get money out of you – that has a tendency to make *some* of them dishonest about the payments they will accept.

Throw everything you have available in the budget at the smallest bill until it's gone. Then take the amount you had been sending to the smallest bill, and apply it to the next smallest on the list. Keep that up with each consecutive bill – Dave calls it the "Debt Snowball", because as you pay more bills it accumulates momentum like a snowball rolling downhill. (This book should help you find the extra money to get your snowball rolling.)

Step 3: Save a 3 – 6 month emergency fund. Not 3 – 6 months of income, though that would be nice. 3 – 6 months worth of bills, groceries and gas.

Step 4: start saving 15% of your total income for retirement

Step 5: start college funds for yourself or your children

Step 6: Pay off your mortgage (!)

Step 7: Build wealth!

Imagine just getting to Step 3 for a moment – you have no payments except for your home, utilities, groceries and gas, and you have money in the bank in case something happens. No more sleepless nights, wondering how you're going to juggle this months' bills. No more screening your calls for bill collectors. No more feeling like you're living a lie, going out to lunches you can't afford to "keep up appearances" with your old friends (who may just be as bad off as you are, but would never admit it!).

A quick note – there are critics of this plan who say it isn't realistic. That sometimes a crisis happens and there's no way to dig back out, because the hole is just too deep. You know what? They're right. When you look over your budget, if you're not earning enough to pay your living expenses and make your payments, and you can't see a way to close the gap, you may be in over your head. If you're that far gone, consider seeking the help of a bankruptcy attorney. Just remember that certain kinds of debt, like student loans and child support, can NOT be discharged in bankruptcy. For everything else, the bankruptcy will clear the debt – then you have to start fresh. It's a huge, overhauling step that you can't repeat for 7 years, so I beg you not to take bankruptcy lightly.

So, now what?

The first step is admitting there is a problem – you bought the book (thanks for that, by the way!) so you obviously want to move forward in tackling this problem. For you veteran savers looking for new saver tips, there will be some things you've seen elsewhere, but I hope you'll find new, challenging information here. After all, this book is called Hard Core Poor – the newbies will find mainstream advice, but I've put in as much "extreme" in here as I can find. Why? You may not use the most extreme advice, (and then again you may!) but it will get your mind thinking in new directions. You might not ever consider using "Family Cloth" in place of toilet paper, for example, but it might encourage you to think of using rags instead of paper towels when cleaning up a mess. The longer you live the Hard Core Poor lifestyle, the more your creativity will be tested and stretched. That's what books like these are wonderful for – sometimes your creativity just needs a little spark!

The big thing to remember is that you're trying to get the most benefit out of the money you have. That can mean different things to different people – you might jump to buy a $110 programmable crock-pot that will allow you to cook dinners while you're at work, which will help you save money on take-out or convenience foods. You might buy a $119 Kindle so you can read library books and free offerings, and clear out overloaded bookshelves in your house. You might spend $430 to buy 2 dozen top-of-the-line, easy-to-use, adjustable size cloth diapers in order to save thousands on disposable diapers. Some expenses will help you save money, some will cost you – if you decide you don't like the taste of crock-pot cooked meat, you prefer "real" paper books, or you can't bear to wash those cloth diapers, then you've fooled yourself and those money savers actually cost you. So in reading these suggestions, do your research before buying something. Ask friends (in person or online) what they think of purchases, and if possible ask if you can see and hold them first. Buy a $5 used crock-pot first, or borrow a friends Kindle for an hour. Hold a baby wearing a cloth diaper, and maybe change the baby.

And give it an honest chance! You might be surprised at how easy these things are!

Clutter busting

One of the greatest truths I've found in people who have money troubles, is that they usually also have clutter. It might just be a little clutter in the drawers, under the beds, or stuffed in a closet, or it may have overtaken whole rooms in your home. (I'm guilty, though I fight it as much as I can and it's mostly corners and closets, not rooms!) It's more than just stuff, though - clutter costs you money. Now, how does clutter cost money, other than having bought the items in the first place? Have you ever bought something, forgot you had it (or lost it in the piles of rubble) and rather than finding it, bought another one? Do you end up with lots of library fines because you can't find the books to return, or worse – do you pay late fees on bills because you lost track of them? Does your home have more bedrooms than people just so you'll have room for your stuff? Do you rent a storage unit? Have you bought so-called space solution items like Space Bags or the Wonder Hangers and still had a crammed full closet? Have you ever lost actual money in the piles? (Don't laugh – one de-cluttering session at a friends home turned up an uncashed paycheck from a year prior. They were able to get it re-issued and cashed, a huge relief as they were very strapped at the time. Another time I rolled over $200 in coins that had been piling up in a house I was cleaning. The homeowners were tickled pink.) Your stuff is sucking money from you!

There's a psychological angle here, too. If your home or car is a cluttered mess, you feel "less than". You *feel* poor. It makes you feel poor in spirit, and you end up trying to compensate by treating yourself to things that make you feel dignified and special, or will help you mentally escape your surroundings. Things like that new pair of shoes, a new golf club, or a new book or DVD. But nothing can help you keep that feeling when you walk into your home and instead of having a beautiful home, you have a cluttered wreck.

It's an awful cycle, which begins with mindless or wishful shopping.

Do you know what I mean by wishful shopping? It's that frame of mind you get into as you walk through a store and spot, say, a fancy new bicycle. It's beautiful, shiny, and you start visualizing yourself on

Saturday bike rides, maybe past a flower stand where you buy a bouquet and carry it home in your bike basket. Maybe commuting to your job by bike – you'll save gas and lose weight! What a great idea! Why shouldn't you buy that bike, with such good reasons like that?

But you just described a commercial. What if you don't usually like to ride a bike, your home is not anywhere near a good bike trail (let alone a flower stall), you work too far away to reasonably commute by bike, and you don't like arriving at work sweaty? Here is the problem. **Buying a bike will not change you into a person who *rides* a bike.** Obviously, this is just one instance – this applies to fancy cookware, craft supplies, guitars, photography equipment, cocktail dresses, etc. **Buying the gear will not transform you into someone who will use the gear.**

This is the first step to break in clutter busting, and often the hardest. We all want to believe that we are capable of instant change, and all we need to do is buy something that will help us change and our whole lives will turn around. That's a tough illusion to give up. Be brutally honest with yourself – are you really going to use that? I once asked a friend if I could have her year-old, still-in-box $5 exercise ball. I had been using one for a desk chair in an office and liked it so much that I wanted one for home too. (We're close enough that usually a request like that would not be a problem.) She said "No, I'm going to use it someday!" Another year later, and her exercise ball has still never been taken out of the box and inflated. My guess is she will **never** use that exercise ball, but she doesn't want to part with what it symbolizes – the idea that she will change into someone who uses an exercise ball.

And you need to apply this question no matter what the price level is on an item. If you're not going to use that bed frame, I don't care if it's sitting like a shiny jewel on the side of the road! If you see something free and it's beautiful and the trash truck will be there any minute, take it to Salvation Army or another charity. The money it raises will help the less fortunate and the item will be bought by a family that WILL use it. Or if things are tight and you need to get your debt snowball rolling, advertise the item on craigslist for a few dollars (after all, you got it for free), but sell it and get it out of your home quickly! Don't let it sit around waiting for a yard sale that you might organize in the next 6 months!

The second step is to go through the items that have piled up around you, and determine what you really need. William Morris, a renowned British poet, once said "Have nothing in your house that you do not know to be useful or believe to be beautiful". As you pick up each item, ask yourself "Do I use this? Is it a decorative item or small memento (that I have a space for)?" If the answer to both questions is no, then why are you keeping it?

"But what about that rocking chair that Grandma gave me? Or my dad's desk – I know it's huge, but I have all these memories of him sitting at that desk, and I don't know if I can get rid of it!" I know. Memories are precious. But remember this: getting rid of the item doesn't mean you're getting rid of the memory. Nothing can take the memories away. If you feel like you absolutely need a link to that item, take a picture of yourself sitting at the desk or in Grandma's rocker. I give you permission to donate anything that is in your way and not being used. Photos are much easier to store than a drafting table!

If it's a non-sentimental item and you're struggling, remind yourself why you're not using it. I've helped people de-clutter before who say "Oh, if I had known where that was, I would have used it!". My comeback to this is always "You *would have* known where that was *if* you were going to use it, because it would be too important to lose." You might have been suckered in at that Tupperware party by all the fancy storage containers, but if you find yourself eating the cereal straight from the box, or using the pasta right out of the package because the canisters are cumbersome, it's time to add them to the yard sale piles.

When it comes to practical items like clothes, shampoo, cleaning supplies, toilet paper, paper towels and so on, it's OK to have spares IF you have room for them. In other words, if you're in a small home with limited closet space, go for the 12 pack of toilet paper rather than a whole pallet. Spares in clothing mean a few sizes up for kids, and a size up and a size down for grown-ups to allow for weight gain/loss. It does NOT mean holding on to your 15 year old child's baby clothes in case you might have another child... or grandchild. Let someone else benefit from those baby clothes – you'll get good karma out of it!

Once you have gone through your first wave of de-cluttering – and there are always multiple waves of de-cluttering – you can have a yard sale, advertise your items on craigslist, or give them to a trusted charity. Use that yard sale or craigslist money toward your beginner emergency fund or your debt snowball, but don't hold onto those items holding out for a higher price. Sell them at a good but low price so they go quickly and don't take up space in your home anymore. If they just won't move even at a low, fair price, donate them. They're just things – they're not worth the space and mental peace that they're robbing from you. Get the stuff out of there and make room for your life!

Housing

Whether you're a single person, in a relationship, or have a full blown family with kids, you can save on your housing.

First, if you have kids, let me reassure you that two kids of the same gender will not die if forced to share a room. If the children are very young, both boys and girls can share a bedroom too – babies and toddlers don't care! Our parents knew this, since many of them grew up sharing a bedroom with a brother or sister (or two). My dad grew up in half a duplex as the oldest of 6 kids (5 boys, 1 girl). My grandparents slept on a fold out couch in the living room for 10 years to free up the two bedrooms. Granted, as soon as they could afford it they moved to a larger house, but they made do until then.

Bunk beds will help free up space, and they even make triple decker bunk beds that will give you the extra sleeping and living space that you need. Standard double bunk beds are available nearly everywhere and start at $200, though the cheaper sets are usually a little flimsy. If you spend a little extra, you'll be assured of the beds lasting until you're ready to re-sell them. Triple bunks start at around $700, and are mostly available online or from specialty furniture stores. If you or a family member feel confident in your construction skills, building plans for double and triple bunks are for sale online for $10 - $25, and you can have a well-built set of bunks for the cost of lumber and screws, usually $100 - $200.

If you have people share rooms, and privacy is an issue (as with an autistic child who may get over stimulated, or with a teen who just needs a little private space), bed tents that fit over a mattress may be a helpful stopgap solution. Children's versions are available for $20 or so, but PrivacyPop.com makes grown-up sized bed tents for bed sizes twin, twin bunk bed, twin XL, full and queen for about $120 - $160 dollars – not cheap, but cheaper than getting a larger home. With these, it's even possible for a whole family to share one (large) bedroom and still have privacy for each person. As a bonus, in chilly weather they help keep out drafts.

Conventional wisdom says it's wiser to buy a home than to rent, and in some cases that can be true. In 2014, several years after the real estate market crash, it's still considered to be a buyers market in many areas – the houses are priced lower than they have been in years, and interest rates are a bargain. It's a great time to get started as a homeowner if you can get a loan.

That said, if you own your home, you will have a lot more bills than just the mortgage and insurance. If something breaks, you're on the hook to repair or replace it. First time homebuyers often think that if they can afford to pay $800 in rent, they can afford an $800 mortgage, but you really need more wiggle room in your budget than that. Why? Imagine the oven just died, you're being cited by the neighborhood authority because your paint is peeling and you need to repaint, and the furnace smells funny. Oh, and the mortgage payment is due that week, too. (I love owning our home, but there are weeks where I wish I could call a landlord to come in and repair everything!) Renting has its' own problems, but there is something to be said for not having surprise housing expenses pop up.

If you're single or even if you're a couple, house-sharing can be a great way to keep your costs low. Naturally, you'll want to room with people you get along with – everyone has a crazy roommate story from their early twenties. But if you're able to find a nice sized place and split the cost with trusted roommates, you can afford much more space and possibly a better location than you would otherwise. Make sure all roommates are in agreement about the use of "public" space, division of utilities, storage in the bathrooms, and how to handle food preparation (do you want to cook together and share food, or each make your own and clean up after).

It may sound strange, but even families and single parents can benefit from house-sharing! In fact, there's a "matchmaking" service called Co-Abode that helps single mothers find other single mothers to share a home. They help split the cost of the home, and they provide each other with parenting back-up when one might be running late and the school bus is coming. On their website, they say:
We present you with opportunities so you can:

afford a **better house or apartment**, within a **safer school district**

halve the cost of rent and overhead expenses, freeing up much needed resources

lighten the burden of daily chores such as cooking, grocery shopping, laundry, homework, carpooling and child supervisions so that you are **less tired and stressed out** and **better able to provide for your kids and** *yourself*

divorced moms can **hang on to the family home** by bringing in a mom roommate to **help cover expenses**

give those in abusive situations support and strength so they can escape knowing there is another mom there to **pool resources with and get emotional support** (pulled from Coabode.com, November 2012)

It goes without saying, if you're sharing a home with a person that will now have access to your child, you want to take even more precautions in screening this person than you would otherwise. But if you find another parent or family that you click with, the benefits (both financial and psychological) can be outstanding.

Many people in the Depression era made ends meet and kept their homes by taking in borders, otherwise known as renting out their spare bedrooms. Back then, food was considered part of the package included in their rent – you can decide whether you would like to include a border in your meal planning. If the tenant that joins your home works a similar schedule and shares a similar diet, maybe you can consider charging slightly more for their rent in exchange for meals. It really doesn't cost that much more to grill an extra chicken breast or make a bigger stack of pancakes, so the extra money could help you stretch your grocery budget a little further. However, if the tenant works a funky schedule, where they never know if they'll be home for dinner from one week to the next, in the interest of fairness you may want to charge them less and clear a spot in the fridge and pantry for the food they'll buy.

The mantra in any real estate, whether renting or buying, is always location, location, location. You can always spruce up a shabby home or apartment, but there is very little you can do about a shabby neighborhood or school system. Find the most affordable place in the right area, going smaller than your preference if you have to, and do what you can to make it your home.

What do I mean by "smaller than your preference"? Think of all those "small space solution" episodes of Oprah or shows on HGTV – most of us can live comfortably in less space than we do. It's mostly a matter of organization and keeping clutter to a minimum. If you've already purged your home of excess, you may already feel like your existing space is much larger. (I always feel that way when the large baby gear is outgrown – when you're no longer tripping over that baby swing, your house feels bigger!) The extreme end of this is living in a "tiny house", less than 200 square feet and often built on a flat trailer bed to get around house building codes. They usually have just a bed in a loft, a kitchenette, some form of bathroom, a small living space, and some cupboards and nooks for storage. Like I said, it's extreme, and not for everyone. But if you're OK living in a space less than the size of a one car garage, you can save a LOT of money doing so. The utilities for a "tiny house" can be $40 or less a month!

If you're renting, make sure the landlord is a reasonable person to deal with. Always clear any major changes that you'd like to make to the property with the owner first – for example, a coat of light-colored neutral paint is usually OK with landlords, because it can easily be re-painted and covered easily. If you decide to paint the walls dark red, your landlord might take the cost of the vast amounts of primer, paint and labor it will take to bring the walls back to a neutral shade right out of your security deposit. That said, if you agree to take care of any maintenance required on your rented property, like managing small leaks, gardening, fixing stuck windows, etc., your landlord may agree to cut you a break on your rent. Save the receipt for any materials you buy for improving the property and turn them in for a credit on your rent – the landlord will also be able to use the receipts as a tax deduction, so everyone wins!

Our house story is an interesting one, but not one everyone can do. I'll share it though, so you can see if any ideas might help you along. First, I had nothing to do with the house that we own. My beloved husband the electrician bought it as a project several years before we met, at a bargain. It was in awful shape, so he stripped the house down to the studs, re-roofed it, hung and finished drywall, re-plumbed the bathroom, fitted out the kitchen… you get the idea. Most of the fixtures were bought from craigslist or were discounted at Home Depot. An enormous amount of work went into our house, most of it completed before he ever lived in it. In fact, the first night he slept in our house was after we were married! The combined total of the mortgage payment (15 year, fixed rate) and the home equity loan payment he took out to pay for building materials were just over $600 a month. Due to the feast or famine nature of construction jobs, he was frequently laid off and on unemployment for months at a time, but he made sure that his bills never were more than his unemployment income. When we got married and became an instant family with my two older kids, the fact that he had always kept expenses low was a huge blessing. When he was working, we paid extra on our debts (not including the mortgage), when he wasn't we simply paid the "standard" payment. After 4 years of marriage, the house is NEARLY done and he has thankfully found a steady maintenance job, which is a huge relief in the planning and budgeting part of our lives. Through extra payments and a small inheritance, we were fortunate enough to be able to pay off our home six years early, so now our only housing-related bills are our utilities, insurance, and taxes.

Your situation might be different – you might not have enough money for a down payment on a bargain home, or the construction savvy to make it just the way you want it. Some construction skills are easy to pick up and some bargain homes might only need basic fixes (along with cleaning and paint). We live in the age of youtube instruction videos – you can do more repairs than you think! Always check with a home inspector or a very wise friend with a construction background to make sure your potential home is structurally sound.

If you find a nice house but the kitchen or bathroom needs heavy work, you might want to ask a friend with a camper if they want a free place to store it (in your driveway) in exchange for the use of the campers' facilities while yours are being repaired. Obviously, you should pay for the use of any propane or pumping out the waste water tank when you're done, but it will still work out cheaper than a week in a motel room. This idea helped us a lot in the first few days of living in our home – our kitchen and bathroom were all set, but carpet was going to be installed in a few days and we didn't want to move furniture in until it was installed. For a few days we ran an extension cord out to a pop-up camper in our driveway and slept there, using a space heater when it got too chilly and running indoors to use the bathroom. It was an OK temporary solution, and the kids thought it was a neat adventure – we grown-ups were more than ready for our real beds, but we got through.

In the Hard Core Poor realm of possibilities for housing, long term camper living (long term being more than a few months) is one way to get by when your income and expenses have stopped meeting in the middle. Anyone living this way will tell you it's not ideal – campers are really not built for continuous use, and the floors tend to break down a lot sooner than they should. However, it's a roof, kitchen, bathroom, bed, and lockable doors when you need it – much better than a lot of other options when you're faced with potential homelessness. You can park your camper on a cheap plot of land, a rented campsite, an accommodating relatives' backyard – just make sure you're not breaking any laws by setting up housekeeping and ALWAYS dump your waste water tank legally. A note on "official" campsites - some campsites have no problem with long term campers, others require campers to move every 6 (or so) days, which can be a pain if you don't have a way to move your camper. Call ahead, ask the owners, double check everything. When things are that tight, the last thing you need is a fine.

Some people decide that the road is calling, and live in an RV or tow-behind camper for the fun of it! (It can work out cheaper than standard housing, as well.) I've read accounts of parents homeschooling (roadschooling) their kids as they travel the countryside, seeing the places they're studying. It doesn't work for all people, since you need to either have a portable source of income (sales, telecommuting) or a pension-type payment to help with expenses. Most on-the-road families rent storage space for their out of season items in a "home" town (usually near family), touching base every few months to restock, store away unused items, and get caught up on dentist and doctor visits. There's a neat service called Virtual Post Mail that will set up a mailing address, open your mail for you and email scans of the mail to you, deposit your checks into your account, and occasionally send a large packet of received mail to you in person. I personally would be a little concerned about privacy, but I suppose it's no different than having a gmail account where they base the ads off of the content of your emails.

If you find yourself in a situation where you have land to live on but no structure or camper, tent living may be your best option until you can build a better home. If you can manage constructing a tipi (there are online instructions all over the internet), it's the easiest to keep warm or cool, since you can build a fire inside or roll up the bottom edges to get a breeze. Commercially made versions are pricey, but it's possible to make your own with a few canvas tarps and long poles. There are actual people who live in tipis, and they enjoy it so much they say they would never go back to "house" living. Other people HAVE lived in tipis, and were more than happy when their homes were built and ready.

Another potential option is an army surplus tent – you can even order a small metal wood stove and stove pipe that's designed to fit through an opening in the tent roof. Think of the tents from M*A*S*H. The tents are made to last for ages, and they offer a pretty fair amount of space with plenty of headroom, and it's possible to divide up the tent for privacy. These are often available for less than a thousand dollars online, complete with heavy wood supports, tie-down ropes, and stakes. Of the "tent living" options, this is the one I would choose.

The most expensive "temporary" option that I've found is a yurt – based on Mongolian portable homes. It's a round structure with a collapsible lattice wall and a roof with an open ring at the top. They come in sizes from 12 feet to 30 feet in diameter, and tend to run in the $6000 to $15,000 range. Some people live in yurts permanently, constructing them on decking or a poured cement slab.

Obviously tipis, army tents and yurts are more expensive than a standard tent, but they come with the advantage of durability, the ability to set up heating/cooking implements indoors, and they're large enough that even tall people can stand up and walk around in them.

Regular camping tents are good for several months or longer with good care. They'll keep you and your things dry and safe from bugs, which is the most you can ask for of a standard camping tent. The main thing I have to caution you about is, no matter how tempting it is or how cold you are, PLEASE do not EVER use a propane heater inside a nylon tent. This is a huge fire risk, and I personally knew a homeless man who was burnt over 40% of his body when his sleeping bag and tent caught fire. Use hot water bottles, heated bricks from next to the campfire, or chemical heat packs in a sleeping bag instead.

If things have gotten to the point where you need to live in a camper, tent or car, please understand that you are not alone. Due to runs of back luck, weak job markets, health struggles and other problems, people who you would never have imagined have found themselves living in situations they would have laughed at a year before. Parents have lived in campers with their children to avoid splitting up the family. Other parents have sent their children to live with family while the parents sleep in cars and work long hours, trying to get back on their feet. It's a hard place to be, and I send my prayers for anyone in that situation.

Heating and Cooling

With such a variety of housing types, you can't expect any one-size fits all advice in this category, can you?

Ha! Yes you can, but just one. Conservation will save you the most money, no matter what you live in or what fuel you use to keep your home comfortable. Set the thermostat low (60 - 66 is pretty good) in the winter, high (76 - 80 is usually OK) in the summer. Adjust for your own needs – for example, if there are medically frail people in the house that would have problems with low or high temperatures, keep it comfortable for them. Hospital bills cost a lot more than air conditioning.

To keep a home warm, first it's important to stop as many air leaks as possible. If you have your own home and your windows leak, then we've all heard that you should weather strip your windows. Close any storm windows that you may have as well. Indoor plastic window insulation kits are also helpful – you apply double sided tape all around the window, apply the plastic film, and use a blow dryer to heat and shrink the film until it's drum-tight. The difference it makes with drafts is astounding. Additionally, this method still allows the suns' warming rays to heat your home (if only a degree or two).

However, if you rent, doing any real improvements on the windows is not possible, and some landlords object to the use of tape on their window frames. In that case, you can take fresh pieces of bubble wrap (the kind with the big bubbles work better) and cut to the size of each window pane. Clean the glass well, then mist with plain water and smooth the bubble side of the bubble wrap on the glass. It should stick on its own until you're ready to peel them off, and the added insulation of the trapped air should help keep a little more heat in your home! Note – this may not be a good solution if you have young children. Not just because of the smothering hazard with the plastic, but also because I have not met a kid yet that will leave bubble wrap alone. (pop... pop... pop...)

If you can insulate your home, put as much insulation as you can afford and can physically manage in your roof. You will prevent a tremendous amount of heat (or air conditioning) from escaping. If you go up in your attic and don't see any (or much) insulation, what you're really seeing is money flying out of your roof. If you can't insulate right now (or you rent), the best thing to do is to hearken back to days of yore. Those beautiful tapestries and canopy beds with curtains in ancient castles were not just decorative – they were early insulation! Fabrics will keep your home warm.

Start with draft dodger "snakes" in front of drafty doors and windows – these are fabric tubes filled with stuffing that lay in front of those pesky cracks under windows and doors. They can be made out of old tube socks, panty hose, or tights, sheets sewn into tubes, even old legs of pants! If you fill them with sand or kitty litter, they'll stay in place well and keep the heat inside. You can also stuff them with batting, but they tend to be too lightweight to really settle in and block the cracks unless you have at least a little sand, kitty litter, or dried beans to weigh it down. You can also roll towels into a tube and wrap them with yarn or rubber bands as a temporary solution.

Thick, insulated curtains are a treasure – but you don't have to pay top dollar for fancy insulated drapes. During the summer, scout the yard sales and thrift stores for nice looking heavy blankets, non-antique quilts, and bedspreads to make "window quilts". Depending on the width of the blanket and the window, you might be able to make several windows worth of curtains out of one pretty quilted bedspread. Sewing these is simple, by the way – it's nothing but straight stitches and seams on all four sides, and a pocket or tabs at the top for the curtain rod. Make sure you have beefy curtain rods that can take the weight – those flimsy metal ones won't last. The blankets can also be used full size to hang over chilly exterior walls as an extra layer of insulation like a tapestry, or hung in doorways or hallways to keep heat from a space heater where you want it. If you're selective and a good shopper, this can look really pretty - it doesn't have to be a bunch of Pokemon blankets all over your home! (Unless you like that. Then – Pikachu all the way, man.) They're useful in the summer too, in keeping out the heat of the sun and keeping the cool night air inside where you want it. People who use these tend to love them, but often mention that they wish they had stuck with lighter colors to keep the place looking brighter.

Carpets and area rugs will help keep your feet warm, as well as minimizing drafts. If you live in a raised home like a mobile home or trailer and the insulation underneath the unit isn't doing the job, a few extra area rugs with foam padding underneath can make a big difference in how comfortable your home is. When your feet are warm, the rest of you stays warmer too, and carpet is a lot warmer to the feet than tile or wood. Carpet is very helpful if you're on the ground floor of a concrete building, too – it will give the floor some much needed additional padding as well as keeping you warm.

Note – several of the heating tips I have are not appropriate for every situation. If you have small children, pets, or other mitigating factors, please use your best discretion when using any of these tips.

As much as possible, use localized heat instead of heating the entire home to the same temperature – it saves a lot of fuel. You can do this several different ways. You can turn down the thermostat and keep an efficient space heater wherever you're spending the most time. If you have forced air heat, there are simple magnetic sheets you can stick over the air vents in your floor, diverting the air away from that room. Space heaters are a frugal friend in the winter – in my experience, the most effective are the ones that look like old-fashioned steam radiators. They're filled with oil, and they heat up slowly but evenly. Since they have no blower, there's no odd, hot draft – just a nice, steady heat. Another nice variety are the infrared heaters (like edenPURE and similar less expensive varieties) – they're more expensive, but they present the lowest risk of fire, making them a safe choice for a kids room.

If the house is getting too chilly, baking a batch of cookies or muffins will warm your kitchen and your belly! The ambient heat from the stove can seriously raise the temperature in and around your kitchen, and your body burns more fuel when trying to keep yourself warm – those bonus calories will help keep you going when you're shoveling snow.

When you take a bath or a shower in the winter, avoid switching on the exhaust fan if it's wired separately from the light – instead, either bathe with the door cracked open or open the door immediately after you're done and dressed. The warm, moist air from your shower will help make your home more comfortable, especially with that awful dry air that the furnace creates. If you don't have kids or pets, try plugging the tub when you shower (or not pulling the plug if you take a bath) and leaving the water in the tub until it cools – the heat from the water will radiate out over the course of a few hours and humidify the air as well.

One of the nicest things when it's cold is to crawl into a nice, warm bed. Unfortunately, if you've been using localized heating techniques to warm the room you're in during the day, by night your bedroom may be downright chilly! If you can invest in a set of flannel or fleece sheets for each bed, it makes a big difference in how warm you feel at night. It cuts down on that initial "shiver time" when you first crawl into bed, too. You can also use a hot water bottle or a hot rice sock to warm the bed before you get in. (To make a hot rice sock, take a mismatched long sock, fill with uncooked rice, and microwave for a minute. It will radiate a gentle warmth for about a half hour – it's good for sore backs, and can also be used as a cold pack if stored in the freezer.) It can be tempting to pile on the blankets when you're cold, but what really keeps you warm is trapped air – if you have too many heavy layers, you may add weight while squishing out that beneficial trapped air. To get the best benefit, use a flannel sheet, a heavy blanket over that, and top with a fluffy comforter. Never lay the heavy blanket over the fluffy comforter – it's like putting canned goods on top of cream puffs. They're not as enjoyable that way.

The oldest and most trusted – and dangerous – method of heating any space is fire. Whether it's a wood stove, fireplace, or even a candle, please take every precaution and keep extinguishing materials close at hand. Smoke detectors are fairly inexpensive and just may save your life – keep at least one in your home near points of fire.

If you live in your own home and it's a location that gets cold in the winter, a wood stove may be one of the best purchases you could possibly make. Wood stoves are expensive new, but there are many used stoves on the market that start around $50. If you're having trouble finding a wood stove in your price range and have some handyman skills, there are kits available from www.lehmans.com that will turn any

55 gallon metal drum with attached ends into a working wood stove. (Lehmans is a supplier for the Amish, so there are loads of interesting self-reliant goodies on that site. They have a lot of items you can't find anywhere else, but some are available at lower prices if you search online. Lehmans is a great place to start for ideas, but research before you buy.) Any used stoves should be checked for warping or holes from overheating and rust, have the fire brick replaced, and make sure the dampers work properly. The door gasket should also be replaced every other year, which is a fairly simple project involving a new gasket, a tube of heat proof cement, and a putty knife to remove the old gasket, all available at your local hardware store.

. A well maintained stove with controlled airflow from the dampers can heat a house all day and night for the cost of your effort in finding and hauling wood. What's more, the top of the stove can be used as... a stove! You can cook anything that you would cook on your range on top of the wood stove in a pot or pan (cast iron is preferable, as it tolerates uneven heat very well). Even if you don't use it all the time, it's valuable in emergencies like a winter power outage. Supplying heat and a way to cook your food? It only takes one winter of rolling blackouts after a blizzard to see the value in THAT! Just one word of caution – it is possible to buy a stove that will heat your home TOO well. Our stove is rated for an 1800sq ft home – our home is 2100 sq ft, but heavily insulated. When we burn starting early in the day, by nightfall it can easily reach 82 degrees inside, even with temps in the teens outside. We may be the only house on the block that opens their windows in the dead of winter!

If your home has a fireplace, you may already have a way to burn wood, but it won't heat your home as efficiently as a wood stove. Most of the heat tends to go straight up the flue, rather than out into the room. There are ways to make a fireplace more efficient, ranging from a simple fireback to a wood stove insert. A fireback dates back to colonial times – they're usually cast iron panels that sit at the back of the fireplace and help "bounce" the heat out into the room. Since it's usually made of thick cast iron, it also absorbs the heat to radiate out slowly, heating the room even after the fire dies down. There are other variations on this concept – one company,

Plow and Hearth, makes a three-sided shiny stainless steel reflector that helps "bounce" the heat AND light. (You can imitate it with three large old cookie sheets covered in aluminum foil and propped behind the fire.) There are also varieties of fire grates (log holders for in the fireplace) that help the air and heat circulate more easily, making the fire easier to tend and pushing more heat into the living space. A full wood stove insert is a real investment and can be difficult to size properly to the fireplace opening, but just like a standard wood stove it will burn slowly, effectively, and will heat a larger space than a basic fireplace.

This next tip is one of those "use your common sense" tips. A lit candle produces a small amount of heat – unscented candles and the liquid paraffin candles used under catering chafing dishes burn hotter and cleaner than scented candles. Most of the time this heat dissipates in the room, making a tiny change in the rooms temperature. However, there is a trick that has been circulating on the internet recently to trap and store the heat so it will last longer. You put a few tea lights or a small jar candle (never a pillar candle without a jar – the heat reflected downward will cause the whole thing to melt into a big, waxy puddle) in a small bread baking pan and put a 6" terra cotta flower pot upside down over them, then put a 8" flower pot over the smaller pot. The theory here is that the ceramic material will store and distribute the heat more evenly. There is a company that makes candle holders with three stacked, graduated flower pots held over the flame like a lampshade. They call it a Kandle Heeter and they run around $30, but they also show you how to make your own on their website, www.heatstick.com . This will NOT fully heat a space, but it will add more warmth to a room, especially a small space like a camper or a chilly bathroom.

I have also heard from people dealing with prolonged winter blackouts that a "canned heat" lit sterno burner or a tuna can filled with Crisco and a wick will help a small room stay warm, if you close the doors or drape blankets at doorways and hallways.

A different neat idea to add some warmth to your home is a low tech solar collector. The concept is simple – find a sunny location, set up a shallow, glass covered box with dark colored metal tubes inside, and channel air through the box. There are lots of designs online, using dark metal rain gutters or soda cans painted flat black, and set in a insulated box topped with glass. For lots of ideas, go to youtube and type in "beer can heat collector" – there will be loads of demonstrations! The simplest solar collector, though, is a South facing window with a large black cookie sheet propped against it. The air should come between the glass and the cookie sheet at the bottom, get warmed, rise, and exit at the top. It may add a few degrees to your room – in any case, it's simple enough that if it doesn't work, you can just take the cookie sheet down and bake with it again.

In the summer, obviously, all these tricks need to be rethought. The trick becomes keeping the cool air in and the heat out, without going broke on air conditioning. We have central air in our house now, but I've lived with no air conditioning, one small window unit for a whole apartment, and several window units for a house here in Pennsylvania. It gets very hot and humid here in the summer, so I do know what it means to be so hot you can't sleep at night.

If you have air conditioning, the first step is to make sure it doesn't have to work very hard. If you can install your A/C unit on the North side of the house, or somewhere where it's in shade part of the day, the compressor will have an easier time cooling your home. Set your unit as warm as you can reasonably live with. Draw your curtains during the day to keep the heat outside where it belongs.

Do as little cooking indoors as possible – cooking on an outdoor grill helps, but a simple solar oven will also help you cook outdoors with minimal effort. A solar oven collects and concentrates the heat of the sun in a small box, so any food placed inside will cook. Solar ovens are available commercially with varying levels of complexity, ranging from what looks like a large silver car windshield protector set around a dark colored pot, to large insulated boxes with gasketed doors and self-leveling oven racks. Even the most basic models, if used properly, will reach temperatures above 200 degrees. Food cooks very slowly in a solar cooker, so load it early in the day and check on it once an hour or so to make sure it's facing the sun properly. I've cooked cubed chicken breast in a hand made solar cooker, and it worked perfectly – we had cooked chicken for our salads, and a cool kitchen.

The cooler you can keep your body, the less you'll need to cool the house, so make good use of cool beverages, cool foods with high water content like melon and cucumber, and wear light, loose, breathable clothing. Since water evaporating takes a lot of heat with it, mist your skin with a cool spray bottle. You're mimicking your natural cooling process (sweating) without getting super stinky or losing too much of your own water and salt. In fact, a popular way to get to sleep in extremely hot climates is to mist your cotton sheets with icy cold water right before lying down for the night. Don't use polyester or microfiber sheets – they just don't breathe.

If you live in a hot, arid climate, you might do well to use a swamp cooler. A swamp cooler, in its' simplest form, is a fan that blows across a bowl or pad of ice water. As the water evaporates, it cools the air that the fan blows, thus reducing the general temperature in the room. Imagine the feeling of a breeze blowing off of a lake – the air feels cooler and fresher because the water cools it. For best results, load the water bowl with ice water and rock salt – salted ice water gets much colder than regular ice water. A fancier version of the DIY swamp cooler is making the rounds on youtube, and it uses a fan, a cooler with two holes cut through it, and ice. The fan is set into one hole, the cool air is forced out of the other hole.

The good news is that swamp coolers are cheap, easy to DIY, and can be operated on a low amount of electricity (unlike an AC unit). The bad news is that they don't work very well in humid conditions, and they can make a space feel a little clammy and cave-like.

Another easy, cheap fix is a wet washcloth to keep you cool. They do tend to drip though, so you might like to check out Chilly Pads from Frogg Toggs – they hold a lot of water without feeling damp, and allow it to evaporate quickly. That means they'll keep you cool with less dripping.

Use physics to keep your home cool – close your windows and shades first thing in the morning to keep the cool night air indoors. At night, open the upstairs or highest windows from the top down (the reverse way you would ordinarily open a window), and the lowest windows in the house, and position fans blowing in at the lowest points and out at the highest points. You'll be following the simple "heat rises" rule, exhausting the heat from your home until it's the same temperature as the night air.

If you have hard floors like wood or tile that are retaining the heat, you can mop them with plain ice water to bring down the temperature a little faster. This is especially helpful in city row home, third floor bedrooms with wood floors. If you cool the floors down, the room temperature will drop enough to let people sleep.

Electricity

Remember Dad yelling "turn off the lights! Do you think I'm made of money"? He's not wrong – turning off the lights will help, but it's not the biggest power saver in your home.

The top ten power suckers in the home change a bit with efficiency ratings, but are usually ranked as - heating systems (electric), cooling systems, electric water heaters, lights, TV, refrigerator/freezers, electric clothes dryers, computers, electric stove and oven, and the microwave.

If your heat system is already installed, and it's electric, I'm very sorry. Unfortunately, electricity is the most expensive way to make heat. If you can switch to natural gas or propane, I recommend it.

The same goes for water heaters, but you can reduce your water heating bill if you lower the temperature of your water tank.

When it comes to cooking, there are cheap and expensive ways to make the same dish. The cheapest method of cooking, in a solar cooker, is not listed here. Solar cookers are free to operate, but in bad weather you need reliable ways to cook.

On the next page I have a table showing the rough costs of cooking using different household appliances.

Obviously these are averages – the price per kilowatt hour or per therm of natural gas may be different where you live, and your appliances may have different efficiency ratings, but let this serve as a general guideline. Smaller electric appliances are going to use less power than a full size electric oven. Even those cute tabletop convection ovens are more energy efficient than a standard electric oven. If you're lucky enough to have a gas cook top and oven, many of these power saving cooking tips will be a wash for you – gas is generally much more cost effective at creating heat.

	Temperature (degrees F)	Time	Energy Used	Cost per unit	Cost
Toaster oven	350	1 hour	0.33 kWh	$.08/kWh	**$0.03**
Microwave oven	High	15 minutes	0.36 kWh	$.08/kWh	**$0.03**
Stove top, electric	High (about 420 F)	1 hour	0.9 kWh	$.08/kWh	**$0.07**
Crockpot	200	7 hours	0.70 kWh	$.08/kWh	**$0.06**
Gas oven	350	1 hour	0.112 therm	$.60/therm	**$0.07**
Electric Convection oven	325	45 minutes	1.39 kWh	$.08/kWh	**$0.11**
Gas oven, electric ignition	350	1 hour	0.112 therm +0.35 kWh	$.60/therm	**$0.07**
Electric oven (standard)	350	1 hour	2.0 kWh	$.08/kWh	**$0.16**

Table from Citizens Campaign for the Environment website

Yes, I know you're not able to make large items like a ham in even the largest toaster oven, but you might be surprised at what you can make combining a crock-pot, large toaster oven, and some form of range like a hot plate or gas burner. You can bake nearly anything from cakes to bread in a toaster oven – you just need to drop the rack to the lowest level and rotate the pans frequently. You can make a whole chicken or ham in a crock-pot for only $.06 in electricity. You can even bake lasagna or bread in a crock-pot!

I know you're just saving pennies here, but if you've committed to eating home-cooked meals to save money, it's valuable to know how much the act of cooking costs and how to save on it. If you make 20 meals a month in the standard electric oven, based on that chart it would cost $3.20 to cook those meals. If you cooked half of those meals in a crock-pot and used a combination of the microwave and toaster oven for the rest, you would only spend $.90 to cook those 20 meals. As a bonus, if you're setting up housekeeping in a camper, tiny house, or any place with an unfinished kitchen, you can have nearly any meal you care to cook with just those appliances – you don't have to live on delivery pizza just because you don't have a full kitchen!

Electric dryers are a huge power hog. We have a gas dryer, but I've had electric dryers before, and I know how much juice they can guzzle. Average dryers use between 1,800 to 5,000 watts, or 1.8 to 5 kilowatt hours. Using the rate of $.08 per kWh, it can cost from $.14 to $.40 per hour to run the dryer – and my loads always took 70 – 80 minutes to dry. So per load it's more like $.18 to $.52, and in my household of five people (one in cloth diapers) I do about 6 – 7 loads a week. Times 4 for a full month, that's 24 – 28 loads, at a cost of $4.32 to $14.56 in electricity. Once again, we're looking at small ways to make a big difference in your final bill for the month. Hanging your clothes to dry will save you more in electricity than using different cooking appliances or even switching off your (energy efficient) lights.

Speaking of lights, Mythbusters proved some years ago that unless you are using 4 foot fluorescent tube lights and returning within thirty seconds, it is more energy efficient to switch off the light when you leave a room. Incandescent bulbs are still available (for now) and cheap, but they use the most power out of all the lighting options and burn out after about 1,200 hours of use. Fluorescent bulbs, both the long tube kind and the compact kind that replace standard bulbs, use much less power and are longer lasting at about 10,000 hours of use, but they also contain mercury, a toxic metal. LED (light emitting diode) bulbs are the most expensive at the register, but use about 80% less power than an incandescent bulb and last for about 50,000 hours before needing to be replaced! The problem with LED lights is that they are directional – they don't cast a glow like the lights we're used to, so they're best suited to task lighting.

Transportation

Getting around, grocery shopping, getting the kids back and forth to school, not to mention going to work – you want the most efficient and inexpensive way to do all these things. But most efficient doesn't always mean a car, and most inexpensive doesn't always mean pulling a little red wagon to the store (unless that sounds like fun to you).

Right away, your location is going to play a huge role in how you approach your transportation. In my hardest of Hard Core Poor days, I lived in a small town in the middle of a lot of farmland. The town itself didn't support many entry level jobs other than retail and food service, so it served as a "bedroom community" for people who commuted to the two larger cities, a half hour drive in either direction. There were a few doctors offices, nursing homes, and a small private college in the town, but that didn't really supply the town with lots of jobs. Because it was so distant from the central transportation hub, there was only one bus every hour in the morning, and then every two hours in the afternoon. There was an Amtrac train station, but trains ran even less frequently than buses and cost much, much more.

People without cars in that town found themselves in a bit of a trap – they could only work within town, and if they weren't internet telecommuting moguls (rare in the early 2000s), that meant working at one of the stores or restaurants for a low wage. That low wage might pay the rent and utilities, but there was usually no wiggle room for a car payment, so you were unable to get a better paying job out of town. In that town, you NEEDED a car.

In other towns and cities, a car is almost an afterthought. You could be within walking distance of several office buildings, two or three grocery stores, the local schools, and a few "fun" places, and not even think about a car all week! To go further distances, a bike, bus, taxi, or car rental might all serve your purposes.

We currently live on the edge of a city. Directly in front of our house is a bus stop, and the road itself is marked as a trail for long distance cyclists. There are 6 restaurants and an ethnic grocery store within easy walking distance. If we had to get my husband to work via the bus it would be stressful, since it would take over an hour and at least one transfer, but it's not a bad neighborhood to be a one car family.

In order to figure out your most effective transportation method, let's look at the various options, what they cost, and how fast they are.

Option #1 – walking. Cost – almost free. You really should have some good shoes, otherwise your feet and knees will pay the price, and a folding shopping cart for $20 helps. Weather-appropriate clothing is also needed. Speed – average walking pace is 3.1 MPH, or a 20 minute mile. That's a reasonable pace that won't get you to work dripping with sweat, unless it's already very hot. Skills needed – you need to be able to walk, of course, but you also need to be able to walk TO work or the store, get through a full shift or shopping trip, and then walk HOME without simply dropping over. Some days this will be easier than others.

Best for – people who have less than 2 miles to go, who have a nearby grocery store. Not ideal for – people who have to drop off children a distance from their job, people who have more than a 5 mile distance to work or school, people who might be expected to give a client a ride somewhere, people with injuries or disabilities, those who live in unsafe areas.

Option #2 – riding a bike
Cost – wildly variable, from free to $3,500+. A used bike can sometimes be found free on craigslist, but the median price for a decent used bike is about $50. Check your local area for groups that help people acquire and repair bikes for no charge. Add-ons like helmets, a lightweight rain suit, lights, fenders (to keep your tires from splashing you), bags and racks for your groceries, and a seat or trailer for a child will drive up the cost, but will make the ride less of a hassle. The high end of the commuter bike line are cargo bikes that allow you to carry passengers and other must-haves with ease. Check out www.xtracycle.com and www.workcycles.com for these high end super bikes. Once you own one, maintenance costs are very low – occasional brake pad or chain replacements. Speed – average slow pedaling pace is 6 – 10 MPH, faster if you're in good shape and not carrying much cargo. Remember – even if you're pedaling slowly, you're still going faster than you would be walking with the same amount of effort. Skills needed – you need to be able to pedal and balance (unless you opt to buy an adult

tricycle, then you just need to pedal), you need to follow the rules of the road, and if carrying children or other cargo you need to be familiar with how that changes the way your bike handles.

Best for – people who enjoy riding outdoors, areas with reasonably safe roads for bike riding (hint – these may be different from the roads you would take in a car – back roads often offer a biker the better ride.) people who don't mind dressing for the weather and packing a change of clothes in case of rain.
Not ideal for – commutes longer than 8 – 10 miles unless you're in very good condition, people with disabilities, areas with dangerous traffic, people transporting newborns, people who hate getting rained on, people living in distant or mountainous areas, people living in dangerous areas.

Fun fact about bikes – for trips in town less than about 6 miles, the bicycle is about as fast as a car simply because you go around the traffic. It's also the most energy efficient mode of transportation when you translate calories burned into an equivalent amount of gasoline energy.

Option #2 ½ - electric bike

Cost – also variable, but there are cheaper models on Amazon for less than $500, up to $4000+

Speed – top speed for the electric motor is capped by law at 20MPH, though if you pedal faster than that it's allowable. Skills needed – all the skills for a regular bike, plus you need to know how to handle the extra power and acceleration the e-boost will give you.

Best for – commuters with a long, hilly ride, people who are committed to using their bike but might not always feel energetic enough to pedal the whole way, people who might be pulling heavy loads like trailers, extra people, or heavy pannier bags. Not ideal for – people with flat, short commutes (not worth the expense), people who are nervous about the speed of the motor, people who bike less than ¼ of their daily commutes.

Side note – I have a cargo bike (actually a trike) that looks something like the old ice cream bikes, but instead of a cooler in front it has a box that carries up to 150 lbs of cargo, and seats and seat belts for up to 4 kids. It also has a rain cover for the kids, allowing me to use it in most weather. I searched all over to find the most affordable version (Virtue brand bikes) and had to buy it three hours out of town because that was the nearest place to get one without having to pay for shipping, and it STILL cost a bit over a thousand dollars.

It sounds like a lot to pay for a bike, especially when $1000 might be really tight, but I bought it because we live within 3 not-very-hilly miles of most places I need to go, and gas at the time was edging toward $4 a gallon. The family van only gets 14.5 MPG, and I wanted to make a commitment to driving it as little as possible to reduce that financial burden. For an extra $600, I could have had an electric pedal assist version that would expand my range and carrying ability, and at that point I would probably only drive the van if it were further than 8 miles or if the weather was terrible.

For someone who wants to ride their bike and expand their kid and stuff carrying capacity, the cheapest and fastest add-on is a simple bike trailer. For as little as $80 you can tote as many as two kids and maybe 4 bags or so of groceries, or as many groceries as you can fit in there if you don't have kids to worry about. Pannier bags, backpacks, baskets, and bungee nets will also let you carry home your groceries without attaching extra wheels to your bike.

Option #3 Motor Scooter or moped (Less than 50cc motor)

Cost – varies, from $1500 to $5000, plus cost of gas, helmets, licensing, upkeep, and insurance. In Pennsylvania, this size scooter does not require a motorcycle license, just a standard drivers license. They're extremely fuel efficient.

Speed – top speeds on these are usually around 35 – 40 MPH
Skills needed – the ability to balance, handle turns, and to know how to generally operate a scooter.

Best for – people traveling on surface roads (not highways), people riding alone or with one adult passenger.

Not ideal for – transporting children, trips that require high speeds, poor weather and visibility conditions.

Option #4 - Motorcycles and motor scooters larger than 50 CC engines.

Cost - $5000 - $20,000+. Gas consumption is usually lower than a car, but is still a factor. Helmets, safety gear (like protective leather clothing) general upkeep, insurance, special motorcycle license and training.

Speed – Standard road speeds, though some scooters top out at 55 MPH

Skills needed – must know how to ride a motorcycle, good reflexes are important since a single rock in the road could toss you.

Good for – adventurous people, people who ride alone, with an adult passenger, or older children in a side car.

Not ideal for – people who are risk-averse, people with very young children, as there are differing laws about how old a motorcycle passenger may be.

Option #5 – public transportation (buses, subways, trolleys)

Cost - $.50 for a short bus ride up to $100 or more for a monthly transit pass, depending on location.

Speed – buses have a reputation for running late because of traffic and frequent stops, but will go at standard road speed. Subways (if available) are fairly fast and less prone to traffic slowdowns.

Skills required – the ability to read and analyze multiple bus schedules, to understand the transfer system and to learn which bus will be the right one, taking you to the right place at the right time. (This is more challenging than the average car driver might guess, and very stressful until you understand the system.) The ability to count exact change also helps.

Good for – anyone living in or near a good sized city willing to wait for the right bus or train, people who live near a good bus route with frequent buses, anyone living in a city with a subway system, parents with one or two children.

Not ideal for – people who may live further from bus routes or have infrequent buses on their route, people who may have serious problems if the bus or train runs late, people who may need to transfer buses more than once to reach their destination, parents with many children (it starts getting expensive).

Option #6 – Personal vehicle (car, van, truck, SUV)

Cost – a reasonably good used car will cost at least $5000 – $7000 - cars are available that cost less, but typically will be in need of serious repairs. The average *new* car payment in the US is $691, the average *used* car payment is between $200 - $350. Annually, operating costs average out to over $9,000 – that includes insurance, gas, tires, maintenance, and depreciation.

Speed – as fast as you dare (remember, speeding tickets are costly!) or as fast as the flow of traffic will allow. A fair average is 20 MPH city, 60 MPH highway.

Skills needed – the ability to drive a car (which includes needing a license).

Good for – people who have long distances to travel daily, people who have many locations to visit daily (like daycare before and after work, banking during lunch, etc.)

People with a strong desire for independent mobility. People who have enough savings or equity in another car so they can either pay cash or have a sizeable down payment on their car.

Not ideal for – people in cities with limited parking, people who may have trouble affording the fuel, upkeep, inspection and insurance, people who live, work and shop within a 2 mile radius.

Option 6 ½ - car sharing programs and rentals

Companies like Zipcar, RelayRides, JustShareIt and Getaround offer short term car rentals for an hourly or daily fee.

Cost – as low as $10.25 for an hour, to $71 for a full day with Zipcar. RelayRides and Getaround have more variable fees, because the vehicles are privately owned by members who set their own fees. They tend to be more in the $30 - $60 a day range, depending on the age and condition of the vehicle. (If you have a clean, reliable vehicle, listing it with a ride sharing company can help pay your car payments and insurance. Check with the companies for more details.) JustShareIt offers hourly to daily rentals, where RelayRides offers rates for a day, week, and month of use.

Speed – standard road speed

Skills needed – the ability to drive a car (which includes needing a license).

Good for – people who usually use other modes of transit but sometimes need a car, like an occasional Costco stock-up run or a trip across town to pick up a free box of kids clothes.

Not ideal for – people who own and drive their own cars (unless you want to list your vehicle as available to rent), people uncomfortable with the idea of renting someone elses' car (Zipcar maintains their own fleet, but is not in all locations).

Obviously, you have to decide what will be the best solution for you and your family. I've come to the conclusion that because of where we live, buying and using a specialty bike is a good use of our transportation money, combined with our regular vehicles. It means that I'll be able to keep my van parked in the driveway more often, a relief, since it currently costs over $60 to fill the tank. For other people, the money I'm spending on my bike would be better used toward a car, since they live far from available work and housing close to work would be too expensive. However, if money is short and moving is in your future, consider how much you could save on transportation related expenses if you lived closer to work, and figure out if you could then afford a higher rent or mortgage payment with the savings.

Another family might look at all the possibilities and decide that a car is the best bang for their buck, since you are not limited by distance, speed, or hills – only by the content of your gas tank.

Food

First of all, learn to cook.

Flippant, aren't I? Learn to cook?

Seriously, though, the more food you prepare yourself, the less you'll spend on it. I'm not saying you should never eat out or use convenience foods, but you'll notice a difference in your grocery bill if you buy fresh meats, fruits and veggies (or at least frozen meats and veggies), dried beans, and starches like rice, potatoes and pastas, and cook them yourself. Simple recipes are fine – we're not trying to win prizes at the county fair or impress foreign dignitaries, we're just feeding our families.

Right off the bat. Give up on brand loyalty. Did you know that store brand groceries are often made in the same factories, with the same ingredients, sometimes even on the same product line as name brand? My favorite money saver store is Aldi. Most everything in Aldi is store brand, it's fresh, my family actually prefers their product, and they have the streamlining a store down to a science. They only stock the fastest selling items. You need eggs? They carry large white eggs by the dozen, one low price. No dithering over medium vs jumbo or brown vs white – you just get their eggs and pay about 30 cents less per dozen than at the other store. Need cereal? Their Honey Nut O's are $1.79 a box. Honey Nut Cheerios cost $3.19 a box at Giant. Grab the box, you don't have to check if it's the right size, because it's the only size. There are 4 – 5 aisles in Aldi – with the smaller size of the store, lower prices, and streamlined choices, I've found it to be the only place I don't mind shopping with three kids or when I'm tired.

I also have to admit, I don't often use coupons for food. Aldi doesn't accept coupons, and often the price for name brand items ***even with the coupon*** is still higher than generic brands. My husband will combine coupons with our supermarket sales to get extra points that discount our gas fill-up, but that's about it.

Our family used to save a LOT of money by going to the local "day old" bread store before we discovered that half of us get serious stomach upsets from gluten. We would fill our freezer for $15, and we got creative. Plain bagels and English muffins became personal pizzas, bread would become French toast, savory breakfast strata, bread pudding... all apart from the usual "bread" uses.

An obvious suggestion in buying food is to buy in bulk, so you save on the per-pound cost of your food. At one point I bought a 25 lb sack of rice, only to be bummed out and disgusted when it became infested with bugs and moisture. Then I learned the secret to longer term grain and dry good storage – 2 liter soda bottles! When a soda bottle is washed well and dried, it's the perfect air- and water-tight storage container for rice, dried beans, or even oatmeal. For things like flour, sugar, and even large bags of cereal like Malt-o-Meal brands,I use food grade buckets with an airtight storage lid. These buckets are often free for the asking at your grocery store bakery – their frosting comes in these 3 to 5 gallon buckets, which are usually discarded when empty. Take them home, wash them and dry them well, cover the sides with contact paper if you want them to look fancy, and you will have a safe place to store bulk amounts of any dry good. (They stack well, so if you're short on kitchen space, two buckets topped with a tablecloth could make a nice end table. Just a thought.)

Growing some of your own fruits, veggies and herbs is a nice way to help stretch your budget while letting you eat much higher quality produce than you can get at most stores. I personally have a black thumb and dislike most raw tomatoes, but I know some gifted gardeners that give me fresh tomatoes in season that taste like candy. If you can plant a pumpkin vine, you not only are able to sell some jack-o-lanterns (a nice little sideline) but you can make some of the best pumpkin pies you've ever tasted. A small package of lettuce seeds can keep you in salad greens all summer long, and one zucchini plant might just produce more zucchini than you can handle. Some of these plants do better in an actual garden, but many will grow just fine in some large pots either outside or near sunny windows.

The one food plant that I've succeeded in making thrive is a small apple tree – I planted it 3 years ago, and this year I got 4 apples on it. Not much, I know, but planting a fruit tree is all about long term planning. In a few more years I'll have a tree that will meet all my apple needs for the fall, when I fill my dehydrator with apple chips and my crock pot with apple butter. Even better? It's a Honeycrisp apple tree, a fancy variety that sells at a higher price in our area. That's really the best part about growing your own foods – you can grow your favorite fancy varieties like romaine or buttercrunch lettuce or spaghetti squash that would usually cost you an arm and a leg at the store, for the cost of your dirt and sweat.

If you or your family likes ethnic foods like Mexican or Asian style food, you're well on your way to saving money. In many ethnic cuisines, meat is used sparingly or not at all, and beans, rice, corn, and veggies are the filling parts of the meal. Pasta dishes and potato based meals are also filling and affordable. A baked potato with some cheese, butter, and a little broccoli or other green veggie is a filling, balanced meal for pennies! If starch-heavy meals bother you, don't worry – you can still feed your family cheaply. Baked squash, sweet potatoes, and carrots, especially in the fall and winter, make very cheap and filling meals that are lower on the glycemic index (won't spike your blood sugar). Possibly the cheapest, easiest, and most versatile food available is the egg. They cook fast, and you can throw nearly anything in the pan with them to help them stretch – leftover veggies, potato, meat, even some salsa and bean dip from a party!

A great way to cook a flavorful soup or stew is French peasant-style, and it begins with something called a mirepoix. This tip comes from www.joyfulmomma.org and her fabulous book about frugal cooking – she not only gives lots of good cooking tips, but reminds you that a cheerful attitude is the best seasoning. I don't know what mirepoix means (I took Spanish as a kid), but what it is is a super cheap, healthy flavor boost for your roast, chicken, or soup. You take a pan (or your empty soup pot, if you're making soup) and drop in a little butter, a shredded carrot, a finely chopped onion, and a finely chopped rib of celery, and brown lightly. If you're a garlic-y family, add a minced clove of garlic, too. Then add the mix to whatever you're making – your food will taste outstanding! It's a great starter for soup, a nice seasoning for your pot roast or your chicken and rice, and you managed to sneak a few more veggies into your diet!

I understand being a single person and not wanting to cook – it almost seems like a waste to go out, buy all those ingredients (because you don't keep that stuff in the house) cook a meal, eat a serving, and pack the rest up for later to eat until you're sick of it. But listen - It's not a waste. Even if you figure out that those TV dinners and frozen pizzas are cheaper than you buying the food and cooking it, it's not a waste. Why? That's lunch on a day that you can't afford to eat out! Dinner when you're tired! That's what big families call "batch cooking" - make 2 or 3 meals out of one round of cooking.

Moms and Dads – I feel your pain. I feel your pain this minute, actually – I'm writing from an after school appointment with my kids, and I'm not sure what to make for dinner tonight. I'm thinking leftovers. (Note – we did have leftovers, and the kids love it because they get to pick their favorites out of the fridge, rather than eating whatever Mom and Dad cooked that night.)

The point is, I know what it's like to be a single mom or a family where both Mom and Dad work, and being exhausted by the time you get home. Homework needs to be done, the baby needs to be changed (and he's teething), and everyone's whining about being hungry. Except the baby – he's just biting people. On those days, it's so easy to look at the other spouse and say "Pizza?". $35 later everyone's fed, but you have the same problem tomorrow night. (What is with these families wanting to eat EVERY DAY? Sheesh!)

In cases like this, two things may help – a Crock-pot and freezer safe containers. If you can spare a few hours out of the week to pre-make dinner for a few nights, it makes a world of difference in your peace of mind. Casseroles, lasagnas, and oven-baked chicken are all great freezer meals, and they can be reheated easily. Crock-pot dinners are so nice, too – turn it on before you leave the house, and you come home to a real home-cooked meal. If you're really pressed for time in the mornings and can't prep a crock pot dinner just then, take a few minutes after you put the kids to bed the night before to chop and season. Put the crock-pot insert in the fridge overnight with tomorrow's dinner in it, then just move the insert from the fridge to the cooker in the morning. (You'll feel so smart!) Crock-pots are also the easiest way to cook dried beans, the mainstay of cheap eats.

If you're really organized, you can make use of "planned leftovers". That's where you make, say, double the chicken you would usually eat the first night, then use the leftover chicken the next night in a casserole or stir fry dish.

People who are really REALLY organized can check out websites like Once a Month

Cooking, that outline menus for the whole month. You spend one day cooking, preparing and freezing meals for the month, then for the next 29 days you only have to remember to take a dinner out to thaw in the morning. I am personally very impressed with people who manage this – I have not yet reached that level of organization, though I would like to give it a try someday.

But why do all this when Dinty Moore and Stauffers have you covered? You can buy frozen lasagnas, beef stew, even trays of mac' and cheese! Why bother making it yourself?

Well, the obvious reasons are cost, taste, and nutritional value. You know it's cheaper to make your own dinner, you can make it just the way you like it, and you know exactly what goes into it. In my family, one of my children and I are gluten intolerant (we can't process the protein found in wheat, rye, or barley), so most "quickie" foods don't work in our household, and those that do are outrageously expensive. So we've had to get pretty good at making gluten-free baked goods, gluten-free pizza crust, and finding the best price on gluten free pastas. It's smarter for us to make our own family size gluten free convenience foods, than to buy the regular version for some family members and buy the gluten free ones for the rest of us.

There's an intangible quality to home cooking, too. The 'Love Factor', if you will. When I was young and single, eating frozen meals and take out, I was existing, not living. I went home to my parents house to have dinner one night, and I was overwhelmed by how I felt after eating a meal that had been cooked for me. My stomach, often unsettled in those days, was fine. I felt cozy. Happy. *Loved.* There is a real difference between eating something mass produced and something cooked by a loved one. The Love Factor. Don't underestimate it.

Clothing

You can have a well-fitting, attractive, in-style wardrobe without breaking the bank! But first – how much clothing is "enough" for a good wardrobe? (I know the answer from many women might be "never enough!") I searched the internet looking for the "enough" wardrobe, and naturally I've come up with rather varied responses. Obviously, a professional working in an office setting will need different styles of clothing than a stay-at-home mother or a 12 year old boy, but there are certain key principles that we can follow for a simple, streamlined wardrobe.

The reason you want to streamline your wardrobe might not make sense at first – it's to help you through the laundry. You might think that having MORE clothes will help with the laundry, since you don't have to wash as often, but do you know what happens then? You don't wash as often. Then you end up with a MOUNTAIN of unwashed clothes, and it feels super overwhelming. Reducing the volume of clothes to about 2 weeks' worth of clothes will give you some variety and help you stay on top of the wash.

In general, you want clothes that will match each other. Remember Garanimals sets from when we were kids? You could buy 4 shirts, 4 bottoms (either pants or skirts), and they would each match with everything else – did you ever thing they were really onto something there? I was blessed enough that with my most recent pregnancy I found a large lot of gently used maternity clothes in my size on craigslist. The woman, a professional office-type who sold me the wardrobe, had very wisely bought all these maternity clothes in coordinating neutral colors with a few accent pieces. Every top could be worn with every bottom, and if I needed a pop of color I could accessorize or wear one of the accent pieces. It's actually the classiest I'd looked in years! (Which means I'd better step up my game now that I'm back into regular clothes, I suppose.)

With standards like that, we can start figuring out what you need of everything. Most people wear their favorite clothes over and over in any case, in about a two week rotation, so I would feel comfortable suggesting a two-week work/play wardrobe for the average person. Note that "outfits" does not mean 10 sets of pants and 10 shirts - the "What Not To Wear" people suggest that you have twice as many tops as you do pants or skirts. This would include

5 – 6 nice work "bottoms" (pants, skirts)

10 – 12 work tops

3 – 4 pairs of jeans or khakis, whatever you prefer for home wear

6 – 8 casual shirts

2 – 3 dressy outfits for special occasions (women may want to have one very nice summer thing, one very nice winter thing, and one that can serve for that spring/fall season. Guys should have one black suit and one other colored suit like navy or gray)

2 – 3 pairs of nice shoes

one pair of kicking around sneakers

If you run/work out, 2 -3 sets of appropriate clothes and a pair of the "good" sneakers

And of course, socks, undies and nightwear (how much you want to have there is between you and your significant other!)

If you're a stay-at-home type or have a uniform to wear to work, increase the proportion of "casual" to "work" clothes, but make sure you have some nice "work" grade items for school conferences and similar adult moments.

That's actually a fairly substantial wardrobe that should serve most people pretty well. This formula works for kids, too. You want to aim for about 2 weeks worth of clothing per person to allow for flexibility in their wardrobe and to give you a little leeway in case you get backed up on the laundry for the week.

So for kids (that aren't spitting up or soiling their clothing on a frequent basis like babies)

8 – 10 pairs of school/play pants

12 – 14 tops

1 – 2 nice outfits

1 pair of school/play sneakers

1 pair of dress shoes

Socks, undies and pajamas

And if you've been shopping ahead at yard sales, it's fine to have all these things in the next size up as well, provided you have the storage space. A wardrobe of that size should fit in one good-sized plastic tote bin.

The average kids' current wardrobe should fit into one medium sized dresser and a little bit of closet space – if you find that those drawers are overflowing, even if everything in there still fits, see if there's a little weeding that can happen of the lesser-worn clothes.

For babies, at least for the first few months, I dress them in those cozy sleepers with sewn-in feet everywhere we go. My philosophy is when it's socially acceptable to sleep anywhere you are, it's also socially acceptable to do so in your jammies! Besides, it saves the trouble of finding and matching those tiny little socks and putting shoes on a child that can't crawl yet. But babies do need a higher volume of clothes than most of us, simply because they leak fluids onto nearly everything, several times a day. Thank goodness you can fit 20 baby outfits into the same amount of space as a pair of mens jeans! Invest in a dozen good drool bibs – you'll save changing their clothes constantly – but fully expect to change your baby's clothes 2 – 3 times more often than older kids. Don't worry – this phase is temporary!

So now that you've analyzed your wardrobe and gotten rid of things that don't fit, are ugly, or you just never wear, what if you find yourself with even less clothing than we suggest? (Check pockets before donating! You don't want to be the person that left a small fortune in a coat pocket and heard about the lucky buyer at Goodwill on the news!) Now you get into the bargain shopping for clothing.

I suggest most of these strategies for baby and child shopping, but they work very well for adult women as well. (I've found that most of these strategies other than shopping the bargain rack do not work very well for adult men, as men have a tendency to wear their clothing until it evaporates somewhere between the washer and dryer.)

You can search yard sales and craigslist for clothes, but I've found it harder to find adult clothing this way – I suggest starting with the thrift stores in your area. I've found beautiful, in-style, gently worn clothing in my local thrift stores for a fraction of what the items cost new. If the thrift stores fail to deliver the things you need, then move up to the consignment stores. Consignment stores are a little more pricey than thrift stores, but the merchandise is usually top-notch and current in style. In fact, when cleaning out your closet, consignment stores are a great place to take your clothes that are still in style and look great, but just don't fit the way you'd like anymore. (Because you've lost so much weight, or at least that's the story we're sticking with.) They'll tag your clothes, hang them for sale, and pay you a percentage of the sale amount after a set amount of time. Then you can use those proceeds to pay for the new clothes that fit you better and make you look fabulous!

And there's the bastion of those who love "new" new clothes but not the new prices – the sales rack! I mention in the kids section that picking out clothes for the next year is tricky when you don't know what size you're going to be in. Thankfully, most adults don't have that problem (unless you just got pregnant – in which case, congratulations!), so you can freely scour the end-of-season sales racks in department stores and T.J. Maxx for savings up to 90% off! And as I mentioned earlier, it's one of very few places that you can be guaranteed to find clothing for grown men at a good price. Just don't get too crazy – remember, even if it's marked down to a dollar, if it's something you won't wear it's still a waste of money and space.

Laundry

Laundry – we all need to do it. Unless you're a nudist (and even then you have towels and sheets), you have things that should be washed on a regular basis. For these purposes, let's assume that you've banished the dry-clean-only clothes, or wear them so infrequently as to make this a minor part of your life. And because this book is called Hard Core Poor, let's start from the ground up – no washer, no dryer.

So, you live in an apartment or home with no washer or dryer, and the laundromat is eating you alive in quarters. Obviously, one of the first suggestions is to buy a used washer and dryer set, or at least a used washer, but for the sake of argument let's say that there's no hookups (or your landlord has banned the portable machines for fear of leaks) and no money for the machines. So, let's move on to the second option: hand washing clothes.

I wouldn't ask you to do anything I haven't done myself. When I was utterly broke back in 2002 and 2003, I not only washed the clothes by hand in a tiny bathroom, I even hand washed *cloth diapers*. I'd have to categorize that as 'not fun', but it did the job.

When deciding to hand wash clothes, it's important to get into a "little bit" mentality. Most people who use a washing machine or go to the Laundromat wait until they have a good load to wash (or 8) before doing laundry. If you're washing by hand, you may want to toss your clothes into the suds bucket every evening and do a "little bit" daily, so the washing doesn't become too heavy a task. If you wash the clothes that you and your family wore that day and hang them overnight, you won't become overwhelmed by the huge laundry piles and get discouraged. Alternatively, you can do as the Amish do and re-wear your clothes (within reason) through the week, then wash them all on wash day. However, you should know that the Amish traditionally do laundry on Monday – right after their day of rest. If you don't have one day a week where you refrain from manual and worldly labor to recharge for the rest of the week, doing a little each day may be a better fit for you.

First, you need three large buckets or rubber tubs – one for soapy water, two for rinse water. You don't need a scrub board, but rubber gloves will save your hands, and a (new) rubber plunger is your key to success. The plunger is the agitator – you plunge it down over the clothes to force the water and soap through the fibers of the clothes. You plunge the clothes in the soapy water (don't use much detergent for this – about a tablespoon or two is enough), squeeze or wring, move to the first rinse, plunge and squeeze, move to the second rinse, plunge and wring out for all you're worth, and hang to dry on hangers, clotheslines, or drying racks. This method of doing clothes is physically taxing, but if it saves you $20 - $30 a visit to the laundromat, it's worth at least trying. If you can't stand the idea of doing your jeans this way, you can at least use it for undies, socks, and t-shirts.

If you're committed to doing the laundry this way for more than a month, I highly recommend a clothes spinner to help extract the water from your clothes so they dry faster. In fact, these are such effective gadgets that you might want to keep them around even after you've bought your washing machine, since they spin at higher speeds and are better at extracting water than the spin cycle of a standard washing machine. Many people who use these can get an additional quart of water out of their top loader machine washed clothes – that's a lot of moisture! In addition to extracting water, it also pulls extra soap residue out of the clothes, so the fabric looks fresher with less dingy residue. There are two sizes commonly sold, and the current prices are $70 - $145. The smaller one holds about 5 adult shirts or one pair of jeans. The larger one will hold about a third of a standard washing machine load.

There are also still hand cranked clothes wringers available, marketed for the Amish population. They are very effective in squeezing out the water, and are great if you're trying to live off the grid, but they are expensive ($150+ at www.bestdryingrack.com) and require a good amount of muscle to wring a pair of jeans. http://www.bestdryingrack.com also sells washtubs and drying racks at better prices than the other carriers, and are the only place online that sells a complete hand powered "washing machine" with a slot-together easily assembled stand, tubs, and wringer. That combo costs $355, but it should last a lifetime.

Now, let's say that you are at least able to get a portable washing machine that hooks up to a standard sink nozzle. Congratulations! Now the only hard part is hanging to dry. I glossed over this part earlier, but hanging clothes to dry is rapidly becoming a lost skill, and knowing how to hang things properly can speed up the drying time and prevent wrinkles.

If you are fortunate enough to have an outdoor clothesline, then this is pretty easy! Get some good clothespins (my favorites are plastic, since they stay cleaner and are easier to spot if you drop them in the grass or dirt). Don't try to get away with simply draping things over the clothesline or tying them on with the arms or legs because you don't have enough clothespins– they WILL blow off, and besides that will take 2 days to dry because they aren't spread out enough. Hang everything upside down. It prevents your shirts from getting funny pinch marks in the shoulders, and the added airflow around the waist area of the pants helps them dry quicker.

No clothesline? Drying racks can be used indoors or outdoors, and work well as long as you drape (yes, you can drape clothes on a rack – the stiff rods make a difference) the clothes so they don't overlap. If you use a rack indoors, place it near your heaters (not too close), your fan or your air conditioner vent – airflow is vital to quick drying clothes. My favorite drying racks are the ones from IKEA – FROST vinyl covered metal drying racks. They collapse down to almost nothing, last for ages, and hold one to two full loads of wash. If you have an older, recalled crib, a lot of people have taken the sides and mounted them near the ceiling on pulleys or hinged them on the wall to drop out and use as drying racks.

What if you're really short on space? Get a tension-mounted shower curtain rod for about $10 and mount it so it's right over the middle of your shower or tub. Hang your wet clothes on hangers (shirts right side up, pants on clippy hangers upside down), hang them on the new rod and flip on the bathroom exhaust fan to move the moisture out of the room. The end result for each of these methods will be clean, dry clothes.

If you're using a washer and dryer, there are tricks for you to save money too! For example, if you can do several loads of laundry back-to-back, the dryer stays warm in between loads and takes less time to dry each consecutive load. You can also line dry clothing, then toss into the dryer for 10 minutes to fluff it up.

What about the detergent? Commercial laundry detergents are nice, but even the bargain priced ones can be too expensive when things are tight. Besides, you don't want to buy a barrel drum of bargain detergent only to find out that your child is allergic and covered in hives! So, use this cheap, easy recipe to make your own detergent. This recipe is all over the 'net, used by countless penny pinchers.

Cheap-o detergent recipe

-Half a bar of your favorite bar soap, grated

-half a cup of Borax (found in the laundry aisle)

-half a cup of WASHING soda (NOT baking soda, also found in the laundry aisle)

Melt the grated soap in a 2 quart pot of water, then stir in the washing soda and borax. When everything is dissolved, pour the pot into a 5 gallon bucket and top off with water. Let the mix sit overnight, and in the morning you'll have a 5 gallon bucket of somewhat gelatinous soap – use a half cup of this soap per regular laundry load, and a quarter cup if you have a HE machine. It really works!

Another alternative to standard laundry

detergent is something called soap nuts or soapberries. The shells of these nuts release saponin, the active ingredient in soap, when they're agitated in warm water. To use them for laundry, you put them in a small cloth bag or a mismatched sock, tie it off, and toss it in with your wash (the suds bucket, if hand washing). You can keep re-using the same 5 or 6 nuts through 7 or more washes, or until the nuts turn grayish and fall apart, which makes them a great money stretcher. They're available online by many commercial names, but I've found them cheaply at an Asian Indian grocery store by the name Aritha Nuts – check locally to see what you can find.

Cleaning Supplies

If you're like most people, the area under your kitchen sink is loaded with "miracle" cleaners. You might have dish soap, dishwasher detergent, oven cleaner, window cleaner, floor cleaner, counter top cleaner, wood cleaner, and stainless steel appliance polish. You might also have disposable sanitizing wipes, disposable floor cleaning pads, and disposable dusters. Most of these are unnecessary.

What do you use to clean then? Baking soda can take the place of most scrubbing products – I find it very helpful on my stove top or counters when they get gunky, and it takes away the ring around the tub like few other things can. Just put a little on a damp cloth and scrub away. Note that I said "a little". If you use too much, you'll spend your time cleaning up your cleaning product.

For the things that need to be shiny, I like 1 part of white vinegar to 3 parts water. It's a streak-free window cleaner, you can use it when mopping the floors, and the mild acidic content will help kill germs while being non-toxic to people and pets. It will also help you see where you left any traces of baking soda – just spritz where you were cleaning, and any remaining baking soda will react to the vinegar and fizz up! If you can't stand the vinegar smell, I've heard of many people using essential oils or soaking fragrant herbs in the vinegar to change the scent. Use your own discretion. You can also use a similar product with lemon juice and water, but I haven't played enough with the formula to make it acidic and effective, but not sticky.

As for the disposable products, we all know they're convenient, but the repeat cost of buying them can eat into your gas money. That doesn't mean that you have to go back to rags for cleaning everything (though rags are terrific), you just need to be smart about how you clean.

Are you hooked on the surface wipes, like Lysol or Clorox wipes? Save the container. Take a roll of good paper towels (like Bounty) and cut them in half with a serrated knife so they're the height of toilet paper rolls. Slide the cardboard roll out of the middle, and put one of the rolls into the saved container. Mix 2 cups of water with 1 tbsp of dish soap and 3 tbsp of vinegar, then pour this mixture into the container. Shake well, let sit for an hour, then pull your first wipe from the middle of the roll. Ta da! Premoistened cleaning wipes!

Maybe the disposable mops are what you enjoy. Yes, they're easy, but did you know that there are mops made to take reusable cloth pads instead of disposable? Use a spray bottle of your favorite floor cleaning mix, spray the floor down, and go over with your cloth pad mop. When it's wet and filthy, pull it off, toss in the hamper, and attach another one. You can even do this with microfiber towels and a standard Swiffer – poke the towel corners into the indentations for the disposable pad – it works great. My favorite "mop" is from a company called Haan – it has a sweeper and steam mop in one, so you don't have to sweep and then mop – it's just one step. It's really nice for homes with small people who like to stomp through the dustpan pile right before you sweep it up!

Do you like Swiffer dusters? Did you know that lambswool dusters are electromagnetically charged? The static will attract the dust just like the fancy disposable dusters, and all you do it shake it outdoors or into a trash bag when you're done. You can also make your own washable duster pads for Swiffer wands out of old flannel sheets –

the instructions are available on www.joyfulmomma.com .

If you change all of these products out for baking soda, vinegar, reusable mop pads and dusters, and make your own cleaning wipes, you could save between $50 - $500 a year, depending on how much you use the wonder cleaners and disposable products.

Beauty and Hygiene

This one is mostly for the ladies, though I know some men who would benefit from this too. The beauty industry in general makes money off of our desire to look 'different'. Whatever our current appearance, there is always something that could be changed (improved?). The easiest way to save money in this department? Go natural.

That doesn't mean you need to stop shaving your legs and underarms like the hippie movement. I'm just saying – if your hair is curly, stop fighting it with blow dryers, relaxers, and flat irons. If your hair is straight, stop perming it. Work **with** your natural texture – you might be amazed at how liberating it is! For curly-headed people, I highly recommend the book "Curly Girl". Written by a curly-headed stylist, she shows you step-by-step how to care for your curls (and even enjoy them!). As a curly-top myself, I spent many years and dollars trying to make the texture of my hair "better", which then meant frizz-free and sleek. Now I rinse well, condition, scrunch and air dry, and my hair has never looked better. I only use shampoo very rarely, and then I condition even more.

On the shampoo topic, no matter what style of hair you have, many people are going "no-poo". That is, they're not using any shampoo at all, just scrubbing their scalp with their fingertips while rinsing. It's a very effective method to stay clean. In fact, people who have greasy hair find that after going no-poo (after a two to three week adjustment period) their scalp balances itself and they stop producing excess oil. I've found that for my curly, dry hair, going no-poo has helped it retain moisture and improved its' overall appearance. If you try this and feel like you're still looking too greasy, most no-poo-ers use a little baking soda instead of shampoo, then rinse with white vinegar.

If you're feeling bold, try aging gracefully! My hero on this topic is Jamie Lee Curtis – she has a beautifully lined face, a great attitude, and a cap of lovely silver hair. She is the queen of aging gracefully, mostly because she went through a bad spell of plastic surgery followed by drug addictions and rehab. She has been quoted as saying "I've had a little plastic surgery. I've had a little lipo. I've had a little Botox. And you know what? None of it works. None of it."

And "Even though women are more educated about it, they don't want to be thought of as having some disorder," she said. "They know these are just images they see in magazines, not real people, because they're all made up. Nonetheless, women continue to hold themselves to that same standard, that ideal of beauty in general."

The point here is, we don't need to look close-up ready. Even the stars aren't close-up ready – makeup, lighting, poses and photoshop change everything. We can (and should) look clean, put-together, and neat; most of us don't need to look like Angelina Jolie on a daily basis.

For general hygiene products, this is the only time I highly recommend coupon use. Most of the time food coupons are for brand-name items that I never buy, because the generics are cheaper than the brand name with a coupon. But toiletries are something else altogether – they don't readily expire, and very often they go on sale. If you collect coupons and watch the sales fliers, you'll find that an item like Crest toothpaste will put out a $1 off coupon in a particular week, and the price of Crest at the store will be maybe $2.49 that week. But if you hold onto that coupon for about 3 or 4 weeks, that's when the toothpaste will go on sale for $1 a tube, giving you free toothpaste. I've generally found (especially with CVS) that the coupon/sales cycle is about 3 – 4 weeks, meaning they issue the coupons about 3 or 4 weeks before the item goes on sale, so if you are thinking of using coupons to build up your stash of shampoo and deodorant, start saving them a few weeks ahead of your first planned shopping trip.

Another thing – the sales cycles tend to run between 6 – 8 weeks apart, meaning you'll probably only be able to stock up on that particular item once every two months. The wise move here is to buy AT LEAST enough to carry your family until the next sale, so you don't run out and have to buy shampoo or toilet paper at retail price. I'm blessed with a mother-in-law who has made toiletry coupon shopping her hobby, so we have not had to buy hygiene products or paper products since we got married – she gets them for free or gets paid to carry them out the door, and then we go "shopping" at her house. It helps that we're not brand loyal or terribly finicky about the kinds of products we use, since she gets a wide variety with her coupons. Since not everyone has a mother-in-law like this, I think it's great to learn how to coupon for yourselves – then maybe your friends and family can "shop" at your house and you'll be blessing others!

GIRL STUFF ALERT – GUYS, SKIP THE NEXT SECTION!

Feminine products, particularly, are a good place to save. Most of us have grown up with disposable pads and tampons, and you can certainly use coupons to get these free or very cheap. I would not be doing my Hard Core Poor job, however, if I didn't tell you about some of the alternatives to disposable pads and tampons. Yes, some women use *washable pads!* No, they're not nearly as gross as you might think, though they do need to be washed after being used. There are lots of companies that make these very soft, comfortable pads, like Luna Pads and Glad Rags, and they snap around the crotch of your undies like a standard pad with wings. They are washed first in cold, then in hot water, and dried however you usually dry your things. Women who use them say that not only are they more comfortable, their cycles are less painful and crampy because they're exposed to fewer chemicals. (Seriously, what is IN those pads, anyway?) You can also sew your own by tracing a maxi pad and using flannel or other cotton fabric. If you use enough layers of cotton you don't need a waterproof layer, but either polar fleece or polyurethane laminate (PUL) fabric, available at Jo-Ann fabrics, are good waterproof layers. There are lots of online patterns and tutorials to help you make your own pads – a quick google search should turn up more ideas than you know what to do with.

Still, those of us that prefer tampons might find this a bit messy – that's OK, there's an alternative for us too! It's called a menstrual cup. Instead of an absorbent item, it's a flexible silicone or rubber cup that you wear internally for up to 12 hours, then empty, wash, and re-use. Because it collects the fluid instead of absorbing it, there is less risk of toxic shock syndrome than with a tampon, and did I mention wearing it up to *12 hours*? Women doctors and nurses, take heed – those long shifts where you can barely dart to the potty might be a little easier with this!

The big name brands are the Diva Cup and the Lunette, which are both made of medical grade silicone, and the Keeper, which is made of natural gum rubber. They can be re-used indefinitely, (the Keeper and Lunette say up to 10 years, though the Diva Cup recommends replacing it annually) can be sterilized between cycles in boiling water, and only cost about $35. The big question is always "how well do they work?", and I can personally testify that I will NEVER go back to disposable products after using my Diva Cup! Once in, I can't feel it at all (I was always "aware" of tampons) and it *never leaks.* I always had leaks with other items! And (not to get too personal, though I'm sure some people are grossed out by now) I know some other women share a problem with... um... personal dryness after their cycle if they use tampons. That's not an issue with a cup, because nothing is in there absorbing all your fluids – it's simply collected and washed away. And just like the cloth pad users, cup users often claim to have a more comfortable cycle because they've reduced their exposure to different chemicals.

There is a learning curve with using a menstrual cup – that first cycle can be a little weird trying to put the cup in right. However, I think it's a lot like learning to use tampons. For most women, tampons were a little weird and scary at first, but once we got the knack of it, it was fine. It's very similar when learning to use the cup – don't let it scare you off, keep trying!

GIRL STUFF OVER – WELCOME BACK, GUYS!

One last note – there are people out there that use something called "family cloth" instead of toilet paper. They keep squares of fabric in a container next to their toilet, use one or two, sometimes moistened, to clean themselves after using the toilet, and deposit into a separate bin to be washed. Enthusiasts say it saves them at least $20 a month, it's more comfortable than even 2-ply quilted stuff, and it keeps their bodies cleaner than regular toilet paper because it can be used wet or dry. If you want to give this a shot, make sure you wash in hot water, use an occasional shot of bleach to keep everything sanitary, and keep a few rolls of standard toilet paper around for company.

Technology

You've just bought a new/new-to-you computer. You take it home, plug it in, fire it up, and decide to write the great American novel, only – horrors! You bought a computer that only has Microsoft Office as a trial download or no writing system at all! In order to have reasonable access to the endless writing and re-writing you need to do (or to work on projects for work, school, etc.) you now have to spend between $120 for the student version all the way up to $500 for the professional version of MS Office. And Norton is set to expire in 30 days – what will you do to protect your computer? Now you have to spend $40 for the antivirus, or as much as $135 for two years of Norton 360. This computer is turning into a money pit, and there's nothing you can do about it! Or is there?

Actually, there are open source software programs that can replace all of those systems for – are you ready for the price? Free.

Some people are put off by the idea of open source software, thinking that it will be too confusing, complex, and will resemble nothing more than lines of code. Don't worry. Open source software often looks just like the commercial counterparts, with the main differences being price and the ability to alter the program if you so choose. In fact, if you've used Firefox as a web browser, you have already started using open source software!

To replace MS Office suite, try LibreOffice. A remarkable open source software program that was developed as an outgrowth from the still available-but-somewhat-older OpenOffice suite, it offers a freeware program that parallels MS Office. You need MS Word? LibreOffice Writer offers nearly all the same functions, fonts, and colors, with only minor differences in the icon placement. If you've gone from MS 2003 to 2007 or beyond, the change to LibreOffice should be negligible. If you need Excel, LibreOffice has Calc. PowerPoint is Impress. To make a database, LibreOffice has Base. You get the idea – each MS program has an LibreOffice corollary. And because the software is open source, it can be (and has been) adapted by tech-savvy individuals to make it more user friendly.

"But wait!" you cry. "My online college/telecommuting job/editor insists that I use MS Office!"

Well, sort of. The point is, they need you to use software that can talk to their software. Which is understandable – there's no point in emailing a file that's the tech equivalent of hoots and clicks to the other computer. The good news is that you can save LibreOffice files in MS Office format! Since this is considered a "standard" email file format, it should remove some objections. All you have to do is click "Save As...", then choose in which format you would like to save your document. You can also use Google Docs to send files to other people, since that's also considered "universal" now.

The bad news is that if other people are going to use your computer, they need to be educated on how to save things properly. And in some cases, re-educated. Ten times. An employer of my mothers' decided to use the old OpenOffice for his staff, and unfortunately my mother had to help several members of the staff save their documents on a regular basis. To be fair, theirs is a health related office and not very computer-dependent for all tasks, so when they used the system they had to re-learn it each time. Still, it's enough to warrant a note taped to the monitor if someone else needs to add a chapter to their great American novel while they're visiting.

If your dean/professor/boss/angelic editor is unsure about bending the rules for software requirements (because of the people that have trouble saving in the right format), offer to send them a sample document from a friends MS Office program and a properly saved one from your LibreOffice program. If they have problems with the LibreOffice version, humbly beg forgiveness (and use of someone elses' computer that has MS Office until you can sell off enough organs to afford your own), but it's unlikely that they'll even be able to tell the difference unless they're told which is which.

Norton and McAfee might have expired on your computer, but that doesn't mean that your system will be infected. AVG and Clamwin, among others, are reliable open source security software programs that will keep your computer squeaky-clean with no financial outlay. Just go to the website and click download.

LibreOffice is a great place to start with open source software – it's clear, familiar, and highly compatible with other systems. But say you need budgeting software? An audio recording program? What if you need an entirely new operating system? We bought a used laptop from our state government surplus store, but it didn't have a hard drive or an operating system. We ordered a hard drive with more memory than the rest of the computers in the house for $50, and installed my favorite operating system, Ubuntu. Ubuntu is a pre-formatted Linux operating system that integrates Firefox and LibreOffice into the program. It's free, intuitive, and beautiful, and it's designed to be user friendly and ready as soon as you download it. Our total cost for getting that computer up and running was about $120, and it's the highest-powered computer in the house.

There are open source software alternatives for most programs, and many people who use them prefer the free programs over the 'brand name' software. Just enter the keywords 'open source' along with the style of software you want into your search engine of choice, and strike a blow for freedom (personal and financial) from expensive software packages!

Entertainment

Ahh, time to relax. You're a smart spender, so you've been watching DVDs and TV from the comfort of your home, rather than going out to the movie theater. You curl up on the couch with a snack, reach for the remote, and encounter... the cable bill. Yeesh, they really charge THAT much for all those channels? There's never anything good on! And under the cable bill is a stack of receipts for the DVDs you bought to enjoy at home. $15 each, and that last movie stunk!

The cheapest thing to do would be to sell the TV entirely, but remember – just because you're Hard Core Poor doesn't mean you have to give up everything you enjoy! Sometimes it just takes a few modifications to make your fun time more wallet friendly.

At-home entertainment can be cheaper than going out to the movie theater, where the $9 ticket price is only the beginning of the charges, and the $5 bucket of soda will cause you to miss half the show when you need to run to the bathroom. (What a curmudgeon I sound like! I actually like the movie theater, but because of the cost I only go about once a year, and then only to matinees.) But as we can see, the cost of at-home fun can be high, too... unless you use a few tricks.

As of this writing in 2014, the average cost for a monthly cable bill is around $71. That's average – some are as low as $50, some people pay over $100! Do you really watch all those channels? If you really get $71 of pleasure each month from your cable, that's great. I'm not here to make you miserable, I'm here to help you save money – if there's a particular program on an obscure cable network that you never want to miss, and that's worth the amount you spend on cable or satellite TV, then go ahead. But before you flip ahead to the next section, consider this: Netflix, HuluPlus, and Amazon Video are all available at a low cost per month, and offer a wide range of movies and past seasons of TV shows. You get to see shows from premium cable/satellite channels without spending the extra surcharges. You can view them on your computer, or on your TV through a gaming system or a device called a Roku box, and all it requires is a steady internet signal.

Netflix streaming service is $7.99 a month, Hulu Plus is $7.99, and Amazon Video comes with a $99 a year Amazon Prime subscription. For my money, Amazon is a great bet – it equals $8.25 a month, offers free two-day shipping on Amazon purchases (which you'll be able to pay for with your swagbucks prizes – more on that later) and now they also offer free 'loans' of best selling books through their Kindle program. The books are credited to your account for a set amount of time, like a library loan, and you don't need a Kindle to read them – just the free Kindle app, which can be read on a smart phone, tablet, or computer.

"But I don't like the movie selection that Netflix carries, and I want to be up-to-date on my favorite shows!" OK, I'll grant you that most of the streaming video selections are limited to movies that we might like, but are not blockbuster hits. And it is true that the TV series are usually one or two seasons old . Of course, once you've stepped away from watching your programs every week, the re-runs don't look that bad, but there is a transition period where you realize that 'everyone else knows what happened to Carrie, and I have to wait two days until Hulu loads that show!' It's OK. It passes. But the various websites – abc.com, cbs.com, and others often upload their prime time hit shows a day or two after they air on regular

TV. Can you wait a day? (I know – it's hard!)

But if you really want a better selection of videos, you can pay-per-download with Amazon (anywhere between $.99 to $5) or you can buy the DVD. Obviously, you can buy DVDs new or used – this is a market that has been around since we were debating the relative merits of VHS and Betamax – but there is a rule for buying videos outright.

Our chief video buying rule is this – unless you have seen the movie and know you like it and want to watch it again, you shouldn't spend your money on buying a copy. If you've seen the movie and liked it, but don't think you plan on re-watching it often, don't buy it. If you haven't seen it and it's sitting in the bargain bin of Walmart, there's probably a reason. You might find something you enjoy for $5, but don't count on it.

In other words, don't buy random movies that will clutter up your space at home once they have been viewed, weighed, measured, and found lacking. If you love the movie, buy it! But don't waste your money and the space in your home (which you also pay for, don't forget) on Bloodsucker Cheerleaders IV just because it was there at the store.

As for watching regular TV, it is still possible to buy a pair of rabbit ears and a digital converter box and hook it to your existing TV. You might pull in 3 – 4 channels or as many as 10 depending on your area for no charge at all, and they usually include NBC, CBS, ABC, FOX, and PBS. Alternatively, you can do what my husband and I did for a time – we negotiated for the smallest, most basic of basic cable. We got about 20 channels in our package for $10 a month. It included local channels, PBS, access to sports games, etc, and for everything else we switched to Netflix. Now we have a bigger package because it worked out cheaper to get both cable and internet than internet alone. Go figure.

Phone

You need a phone. No, you NEED a phone. No kidding around.

There was a time not that long ago that if you lived in a less affluent area, having a phone was ideal, but it wasn't that unusual if you didn't have it. And sometimes the bill was simply out of reach that month, so you took your quarters down to the payphone, let your friends and family know what was going on, and if anyone wanted you they'd have to just stop by. Those days are gone. You need to be reachable by employers, your childs' teacher, and anyone else who might need to contact you in an emergency.

Land lines still exist, and they cost a good bit less than they used to 20 years ago. If all you need is a home phone number, you can get basic local service sometimes as low as $25 a month for a standard landline or $10 a month for a VOiP (voice over internet) unit that uses your internet signal. If you get a standard landline and make your long distance phone calls through Google Voice, a free service through the computer, you won't have long distance charges, and your basic contact requirements are met.

If you need more than a land line, either because constant connectivity is an expectation these days, land lines are limiting, or because you don't live in a home with a wall jack, there are many cell phone plans that won't leave you penniless because you sent too many text messages.

First, there's the pre-paid option. The phones are cheap (sometimes just $10 for a non-smart phone) and you pre-load the phone with minutes bought as needed. It's affordable and you can't go over budget on minutes. The biggest pain with these phones is running out of minutes when you really need to make or receive a call. If you have access to the internet and a debit card, most of the prepaid plans now allow you to buy time online and add it to your account – a nice time saver if you don't want to run to the store to reload your phone.

If you want a more affordable cell service and you can afford to pay more for the phone itself, there's a new variety of cell phone that uses wi-fi signals to send your call when they're available, and cell phone signals when you're away from a hotspot. Currently the only company I'm aware of that offers this service is RePublic Wireless

– they have a few proprietary phones ranging from $99 - $299, which are required for their plan, but then it's only $5 - $45 a month, unlimited talk, text and data. $5 per line is pretty darn cheap, which uses only wifi for calls, text and data. (The $10 a month plan is unlimited talk/text through cell network, and unlimited everything through wifi.) As you go up in plan structures, you get more of your services offered through the cell network as well. The phone price is higher than the prepaid phones, but they're full-service smart phones, and the cheap service could really be worth saving up that cash for the phone.

If none of those options appeal to you, see if you can handle a smaller cell plan with a major carrier and refrain from using data services. Use the cheapest phone available, go over the plans, and see what you can comfortably live with. And does your child REALLY need a cell phone? If your household has a landline, could they do without a cell, at least until they have a method of paying for it themselves? So far, our oldest child is 12, and we've managed to stumble along without her having her own phone. That doesn't mean she hasn't asked for one, but she doesn't have to get everything she asks for. If something changes in the future, we'll look at some of the low-cost options and possibilities, which she will pay for out of her own money.

Internet

The Internet is a must in this society. If you can't access the internet in some way, you're missing out on so many ways to save money, make money, communicate, and just have fun. The question is, how do you want to access it?

The cheapest method is free – use the public library's computer and internet service for your basic job hunting, research, and email needs. It's not the most convenient method of accessing the internet, but it's available to everyone with a library card (which you should get right away, if you don't have one yet).

If you have a laptop with wi-fi connectivity, you can hang out anywhere that offers free wireless internet and do whatever you need to do. Most Starbucks and Panera restaurants offer wi-fi, as well as many McDonalds and hotels.

Maybe you're one of the lucky folks that live in a hot spot provided by a local business, and you decide to piggyback. Note: I am NOT suggesting that you piggyback on someones' personal wi-fi without permission. I'm saying that if a business provides a free hot spot within range of your residence, it's worth asking if they mind you using it as your internet source. Odds are, they're so accustomed to people using it that they'll be touched and pleased that you asked. If they're not OK with you using their internet, or if you're concerned about security while shopping online, you should look into getting your own service.

Check your local area – in certain neighborhoods, you may have a broad selection of internet providers to choose from, or there may be only one game in town. Either way, compare as best you can – it can make the difference between a $40 internet bill and an $80 bill. I've seen as low as $19.95 per month advertised, but when I requested that package, I was told it wasn't available in our area.

If speed is not a major issue, and your home has a land line phone, there are still dial-up internet services you can access for free. You may have to deal with pop-up ads, but free is a hard price to beat. Some of the free services are FreeDialup.org, Fast Free Dialup, and MetConnect. These services are locally based, so you may have to do a little digging to find a service in your area with a local dial up number. If you don't mind paying $9.95 a month, Net Zero's dialup plan may suit your needs with fewer ads and interruptions.

Banking (or how to access your money when the banks won't work with you)

If you have a checking account, savings account, or any other kind of account with a bank, your first task when you get your statement this month is to check how many and what kind of fees they charge for the privilege of accessing your own money. If they charge you when your balance falls below a certain level, if they charge you when you use an ATM that isn't theirs... or sometimes even charging for one that IS theirs, if you pay a fee when using the debit feature instead of credit at the store, write them all down and add them up. That total is now your number to beat. Call around to different banks and credit unions, and find out who has ACTUALLY free checking (not just free on alternate Tuesdays if you have $5000 in the account).

You'll probably have the best luck at finding a free account at a credit union. What's the difference between a bank and a credit union? Banks are profit-driven companies. A credit union is a cooperative financial institution in which individuals pool their money to provide loans and services to other members. In the United States, credit unions are nonprofit groups, and their cooperative structure is designed to ensure fair dealing. That means they typically don't have as many service fees as a profit-driven business.

Credit unions do have requirements to become members, but they're usually not difficult to meet. Our credit union allows you to open an account if you have a family member who has an account, or if your employer, school or other association offers membership as a benefit. Others allow you to join if you live, work or worship in their service area.

The upside of credit unions is they offer personal service and low fees. The downside is because they are small, local institutions, they have fewer ATMs (all of our local credit unions work together, so we can use any credit union ATM with no fee) and limited office hours, and online banking may or may not be available. Banks are everywhere, many have extended office hours and online banking, and there should be an ATM near your home or office.

But this is Hard Core Poor, here. One of the things that has happened to many Hard Core Poor people is an overdraft or "bounced" transaction. If you have a savings account, overdraft protection, or some other cushion, you simply cuss yourself out, deal with the $35 overdraft fee, and move on. But if you don't have any wiggle room in your budget, that $35 fee could mess up your finances for weeks, sometimes even months or years. How?

 Let's say you have $50 in your account, you spend $10 on pizza, $10 on a few staples at the store, and $10 somewhere else on something fun. You pull in at the pump, swipe your card, and space out as you put $40 into your tank. You panic a little, but there's nothing you can do about it now, so you figure you'll make up the single $35 overdraft charge somehow out of your next paycheck. Maybe you'll skimp on a few things next week. The trouble is the bank sends you a notice that you're $90 in the hole! They put through the $40 charge first, then the three $10 charges. You got two $35 overdraft fees instead of one, plus the amount that you actually overcharged. If you don't put money in the account promptly, they charge you another fee for carrying a negative balance! Now imagine that it's a car payment that went through early, and you had no idea as you made six small debit purchases that day. You would have $210 to make up just in fees! If you're living close to the financial edge already, that might be an amount that will cause serious problems for a while. Your whole paycheck might end up just filling that overdraft hole, with nothing left over to live on for the next few weeks. And if your account is left in a negative balance for too long, the bank will close it and put you on a list with CheckSystems, which alerts other banks if you try to open a checking account with them. This is why many people turn to check cashing businesses.

In my Hard Core Poor days, not only did I go through this banking nightmare (thanks to young foolishness and poor record keeping), many of my convenience store co-workers were also in the same pickle. After I cleared my name with the bank, I went a few years without a personal account until I got a job that required me to have a checking account for direct deposit purposes. I found a bank that would agree to give me a checking account, but only after I took a "money-wise" class from the bank manager. Up until then, I managed with either cashing my check at low-fee places, or I went to a bank where I had opened a savings account just so they would cash my paychecks.

Which is - workaround #1 – if the bank won't allow you to open a checking account, see if you can open a fee-free savings account. You might be required to keep a few dollars in there at all times to keep it active, but you would have access to banking facilities when payday rolls around, or if a relative sends you a check for your birthday. (Think about that – your aunt sends you a $50 check for your birthday and you can't do anything with it because you can't deposit it!)

Workaround #2 is to use stores as your check cashing solution. Walmart charges between $3 and $6 to cash a check up to $5,000, and Kmart offers check cashing for less than $1 per check. Check your local areas, you may be able to find similar deals in other large stores. They usually will cash paychecks, government checks and other "official" checks with no trouble. Personal checks are trickier and depend on the site – Kmart will cash a personal check up to $500, but that seems to be the exception rather than the rule.

Last on your list (or anyones list) should be the "Check Cashing Stores!" that are all over the low-income sections of town. They make their money off the backs of the poor by charging crazy fees for cashing their checks. The same check you could cash at a bank for free or Kmart for a dollar, you might have to fork over $6 - $20 just so you can use your money! I know, you might be in a position where you can't even get to Kmart without bus money, and you can't get the bus money until you cash your check. Please try. Keep $5 taped under your bed for moments like this. You shouldn't have to pay $20 to get $500. You can use that $20 elsewhere!

The other obstacle when you don't have a checking account is how to pay your bills. You'll have to use money orders. A money order is like a pre-paid check – it's safe to send through the mail, to pay utilities, mortgages and rent with, and you get a stub with an identifying number for your records. You pay a small fee when getting the money order, between $.49 to $5. U.S. Postal Service money orders are available nationwide and cost $1.25 up to $500, and $1.65 for $500 - $1000. Most supermarkets carry Western Union money orders for varying fees as well. Naturally, if you have several bills to pay, you want the cost per order to be as small as possible. Shop around as much as you reasonably can to avoid paying captive audience pricing at the local corner store.

You can also buy prepaid credit cards either as a Visa gift card or for a dollar fee as a reloadable "credit" card. It's a little easier to pay bills immediately and online with one of these, and you can also make money saving online purchases with these once your immediate financial crisis is over. These are available at Dollar General, most mega stores like Walmart or Target, and places like Family Dollar. They also have a number of "gotcha" fees built in, so research which card will work best for you. The Walmart Card waives reloading fees if you sign up for direct deposit with your paycheck, making the card a very effective substitute for a checking account.

Some people might be aghast at the idea of being "unbanked" and wonder why anyone would bother with all this nonsense. People who grew up with check cashing stands might think this is common knowledge. The fact is there are a lot of people who have unexpectedly fallen off the financial ladder, who never had to deal with banks no longer wanting their business before. They've never looked at the bank teller in shock after learning their paycheck for the last two weeks will be eaten up by overdraft charges, and had to wonder how they'll feed their families. I'm not advocating dodging your responsibilities, but when your check will just barely cover your rent, utilities, and food, and the bank wants it all to cover fees, I am in favor of getting your check cashed elsewhere, ***setting up a payment plan with the bank***, and covering your essentials.

I understand that a lot of people might sneer at this section, saying people brought on this misery themselves. Sure, if everyone were more careful with their book keeping, this wouldn't be a problem. But the trouble is human error. When you have a margin for error, a mistake is minor correction. With no margin for error, a mistake is a catastrophe. And it's hard to see how much of a catastrophe it will be until you make that mistake. I'm not going to scold anyone for making a mistake – they scold themselves just fine - I'm going to try to help them through it so they can come out on the other side a little wiser.

Once you have cleared your account with the bank, ask if you can have access to your account again. No matter how adept you get with workarounds like check cashing, prepaid cards, and money orders, they're still workarounds, and life is complicated enough. The bank may have certain conditions for you to meet to get an account again, like keeping a minimum balance in a linked savings account, or taking a money management class. See what options there are that cost you the least amount of money, and keep careful track of your account. Remember, it's OK to carry cash – cash is easy to keep track of, and it's easy to see when you're running out. Our family pulls out a set amount of gas, grocery, and "whatever" money each payday, and that's all we get until next payday. It helps us stay on track.

Taxes

If you're one of the Hard Core Poor, you probably make enough to file taxes, and little enough that you can get a refund. Some of you may make more money than that – great! You may end up owing something in taxes, but be sure you don't pay a penny more than you owe. For the rest of you:

The Earned Income tax credit pays you more than you paid in for taxes. If you qualify, you can receive an extra sum in your refund check. It's usually thought to be something for parents, since they do get the largest dividends from the credit (as much as an extra $5,000 if you have 2 or more kids) but even low income childless people can benefit from this tax credit. The EIC tax credit is an annual chance for many hardworking people to make a serious change in their lives, by using that money to pay down debts, buy a car, or save for a down payment on a house. Unfortunately, many people don't get the most benefit that they could out of this extra cash. To me, the most frustrating reason for this is the refund anticipation loan.

I am personally begging you – if you go to Jackson Hewitt or Liberty Tax Services, do

NOT request the refund anticipation loan. Don't let them talk you into it. For a charge of $100 - $200 over and above the cost of filing, the tax preparation company will give you the balance of your tax refund immediately. But the trick is, it's a loan. It's not a rapid refund, it's an expensive loan that will charge you 24% APR. H&R Block was banned from offering refund anticipation loans because they were considered predatory lending practices, but other companies are still offering them. These guys set up storefront tax preparation offices everywhere, but it's particularly thick in the low income areas of town. Why? They know that poor people are willing to hand over part of their money so they can get it now and pay for things that have fallen behind. But this is the crazy part – if you e-file, your taxes can be processed in 7 – 10 business days! If you have a checking account (many lower income folks don't) you can get direct deposit within three weeks of filing. People – can it wait three weeks? If you need a check by mail, it can take more like 6 -8 weeks – can you plan ahead for that?

If you can, I encourage you to file your own taxes. Really, if you follow the directions in the 1040 manual step by step, and you don't have any rental property or small business income with payroll taxes, most people should be able to fill out and file their own tax return. It's honestly not as hard as many people think - following the 1040 instruction manual should be boring, but straightforward. Just go step by step and don't jump ahead – I find that people get most confused when they try to do things out of order, like trying to put unemployment compensation in with regular income (it goes in a little later in the form).

If you still don't feel confident enough to do it yourself, or if you have quirky sources of income (like SSDI, unemployment, railroad pension, etc.), there are ways to get filing help for free. In fact, the Welfare department of Pennsylvania offers free tax preparation and filing help to all people who qualify for any variety of Welfare services. TurboTax Online offers free Federal tax prep and e-filing, though you'll still need to do your own state and local returns, or pay for extra software to do the state and local. (Don't – state and local are a breeze compared to federal.)

I've had people ask me "Why should I do my own taxes? I can pay someone to do them and I know they'll be right, and besides, I don't have the time to sit around messing with numbers."

It's your decision, but ponder this for a moment. If you use (free) tax prep software and include everything you'll need in your document pile before you sit down, it should take most people about an hour, maybe two, to do your federal return. (An hour or two! We stress so much about something that only takes an hour or two out of the whole year! Are we nuts or what?) Most tax prep software walks you through your return, so it's unlikely that you'll have a mistake unless you enter something wrong, like reversing numbers. To have your taxes done by a tax preparer, you'll pay anywhere from $50 - $250, depending on how complicated your return is. How much is an hour of your time worth to you? Would you like to be paid $50 - $250 for an hour or two of work? When you do something yourself, rather than paying someone to do it for you, you essentially pay yourself the amount of money that you would have spent. (I like that better than "I saved..." - it really helps you see the value in the work you do for yourself.)

Kids

Yes, kids.

This is going to be the longest segment in the book because kids have so many needs, so I'm going to break it down into subcategories.

I'm not going to try to fool you – kids do cost money. Especially as they get bigger, they can cost you a bundle in food and various activity fees. But kids don't have to cost *more* than adults! In fact, I was profoundly disturbed by a story on the internet – a young couple with a toddler son had sunk into over $12,000 in credit card debt and were 2 weeks behind on their mortgage, claiming that the costs of having their son had devastated them. In looking at the footage of their home, I could see they had spared no expense in decorating their baby's room, they had a smart phone, satellite TV, their baby was toddling around in high-end clothes, and eating pre-packaged toddler snacks. There were tons of places where they could have made up their shortfall! Let's begin with:

Baby needs

If you listen to Babies R Us ads, Target, Child Craft, etc., babies require many things to exist at all – a crib, of course, but also a (matching) changing table, dresser, rocking chair, cradle, coordinated bedding with lamps and wall décor, and curtains. They need a high chair, pack-n-play, exersaucer, walker, Bumbo seat, bouncy seat, motorized swing, and a travel system that includes a $500 stroller and $180 infant car seat. Not to mention the specialized baby bottles, pacifiers, formula, diapers and wipes that you'll have to buy – you do have stock in those companies, right?

Truth – new parents are suckers, and the baby industry knows it. They play on two major facts.

1. New parents are nervous because they want to be the best parents they can be. That means they're more susceptible to ads that say "Your baby needs this, and good parents will make sure their baby gets it."
2. Babies are cute, their stuff is cute, and it's fun to buy cute stuff!

Are they good reasons to buy things? Not really. Just very tempting! So let's run down what your baby actually needs.

Food – if you can do it at all, please breastfeed your baby, and keep it up as long as you can! Even the best formula is not as good for your baby as your own milk. (It reduces your risk of breast cancer and helps you lose those post-pregnancy pounds, too.) It's also the cheapest way to feed your baby – if you're with your baby all the time, you might not even need to get a breast pump! A good pump is a wise investment though, if you plan on spending any time away from your baby. The Medela Pump In Style has long been considered the gold standard in mechanical pumps, especially for moms who pump daily or several times daily. It does run around $270 – a hefty investment, but cheaper than formula feeding. There's another, innovative brand of pump called Freemie, which is giving Medela stiff competition. Instead of having to hold the bottles and flanges with your hands, the Freemie has cups that slip into your bra, and the tubing hangs from the bottom of your shirt. You can then discretely pump (with your shirt on!) with their power unit, their hand pump unit, or hook the tubes to another brand of unit like Ameda or Medela. Their prices are very competitive, with their hand operated system costing only $70 (it pumps both sides at once!) and their electric system only $160. It was developed by a doctor and mother who worked in an emergency room and needed to be able to pump quietly, quickly, discretely, and be able to disconnect from her pumping to handle an emergency at a moments notice.

Some insurance companies will chip in for the cost of a good pump or even cover it completely, so it's worth contacting your insurance company about this – BEFORE you deliver. Many companies will still only cover known name brands like the Medela, but the Freemie is now covered by several insurance companies.

For more occasional pumping, I like the Avent Isis manual pump – it's about $50, available at drugstores like CVS (which means you can use Extra Care Bucks left over from coupon shopping), and rather gentle as far as pumps go. It only pumps one side at a time, however, which means a longer time spent pumping overall.

If you're having trouble nursing your baby, call your insurance company and see if they cover consultations with a lactation specialist. These are people who are specially trained to help women and babies get off to a good start with breast feeding. If your insurance won't cover it, try contacting your local La Leche League – it's a breast feeding support group that can also help you through the tough patches, and they're headed by a trained professional that can help answer your questions. It really is worthwhile for the health of you and your baby (and wallet) to give breastfeeding your best long-term shot!

If you can't breastfeed, that means you'll need formula. Factually speaking, the store brand formula is just as good for your baby as Enfamil or Gerber – they all have to meet certain government-set nutritional standards. Likewise, baby bottles don't have to be super fancy with flow valves to feed your baby – they just have to have the right flow nipple. Obviously, if your baby has trouble with one kind of formula or bottle, by all means change it! But don't start your baby on Nutramigen (very expensive formula) in specialized bottles right off the bat if he or she doesn't need it – start with the basic bottle and silicone nipple, and generic milk-based formula. If there's an issue, talk to your pediatrician to see if the bottle should be changed, or if you should switch to generic soy-based formula. If that doesn't work, then you start changing brands, like Enfamil or Gerber, and formulations, like Nutramigen or Alimentium. If you do use name-brand formula, contact the company and request their promotional pack – usually they'll send at least one free can of sample formula, and lots of coupons. Take advantage of those coupons!

Solid foods

You can puree your own baby food from the food you cook yourself. Veggies, steamed and mashed, are very easy to make. Ripe bananas and avocado don't even need special cooking, just mash well with a spoon! In Mexico, mothers feed their babies well-cooked soft beans or well-cooked rice as first foods. Some moms follow this here, where you just feed the baby soft, small pieces of table food, which is totally OK. Scientists refer to baby food as a perceived social need – for thousands of years humans have managed without strained peas. You won't do your child harm by avoiding purees. For more information on this feeding method, check out the book Baby Led Weaning – it gives you the rundown on how to feed your baby safely on table foods.

Listen to your doctor about when to begin solids – don't try to mix rice cereal in with a two month old baby's formula with the mistaken idea that it will fill the baby's belly so they'll sleep better. It can actually cause tummy troubles, because infant stomachs are not meant to digest anything but breast milk or formula at that age. Most doctors recommend waiting until baby is between 4 – 6 months old before introducing solids. Waiting can be better for your baby's health AND your budget – how many things can you say that about?

Car seat

The only thing I am going to say you really should buy new. Regulations change, seats over 5 years old are "expired", and if it's been in an accident it's no longer considered safe. If you do buy a used one, make sure it's from someone you trust who can guarantee it was never in an accident, check the date of manufacture to make sure it's within dates, and be sure to register it with the manufacturer. There are two basic options when it comes to car seats for your newborn.

Newborn car seats are the ones that you see parents carrying around by the handle or popped into a shopping cart – they have a detachable base that stays in the car, they ONLY are rear-facing, and they typically only hold a baby up to 20lbs. They're very convenient in those first few months while the baby is tiny, but babies have a way of outgrowing those infant seats before they've even reached a year old. They tend to run from between $80 up to over $250, depending on brand.

Infant/toddler car seats are much more practical as a long-term solution – they stay buckled in the car at all times, but they can be rear or front facing and handle much higher ranges of baby weights, from 5lbs sometimes up to 80 lbs! There is only one downside – sometimes, if your baby is very tiny when he or she is born, the hospital will insist that they go home in a newborn seat so that they're supported better. If that happens, you may just have to bite the bullet and invest in the newborn seat, but know that the infant/toddler seat will serve you much longer. They can run anywhere from $45 - $500, depending on how fancy you want to get.

For either kind, if the seat is more than 6 years old (if re-using for another child) or involved in an accident of ANY kind, it should be disposed of.

Clothes

Are you kidding? Do you KNOW how fast babies grow? In second-hand shops, consignment stores, and yard sales, you'll find baby clothes with brand-new tags still on them because the original intended wearer outgrew the clothes before they could be worn. Honestly, other than one or two really cute outfits for pictures and visits to Grandma, I'd recommend getting your entire baby wardrobe secondhand. They don't know what they're wearing – save the money for those teenage years when they start getting picky!

Yard sales can be hit-or-miss, but if you can find a yard sale with baby clothes in the right size range and gender, you've hit a gold mine! You'll usually find the best prices at yard sales, but be wary of the ones that overprice their clothing. They'll try to justify their $5 and $6 per sleeper or outfit prices by explaining how much each one cost new, but remember - it's not your fault they paid $30 for a Hanna Anderson dress, and you don't have to help them recoup their loss. There may be another yard sale down the block that's only asking $.50 - $1.00 per item, and might cut you a deal to fill a bag. Your baby won't mind being in Carters or Old Navy rather than Dolce and Gabbana and Ralph Lauren (but if you find those name brands for a steal, no one needs to know what you paid!).

Craigslist and eBay are something like shopping yard sales, but you get to browse from your computer. The same rules apply to craigslist shopping as yard sales – don't overspend, be patient, inspect things carefully, but if you find a good deal in the right size, jump! (As always, be safe if you're meeting someone from the internet – meet in public and make sure someone knows where you are.)

Thrift stores will cost a little more than your average yard sale, but they offer the advantage of being open year round and usually having a decent selection. You may have to scout the stores in your area to find the ones with the most consistent supply. For example, our go-to store used to be Salvation Army, but a new store called Community Aid opened in our area that had similar low prices, a more reliable supply of the kid sizes I needed, and they only put out the "good stuff", meaning I didn't have to focus so hard on checking for damage or stains. Our local Goodwill has OK merchandise, but I find the prices to be much higher than I want to pay unless I go to their "Bin Store" - they put all the clothing into dump bins and you sort through to find what you want for $.85 a garment. It's a time consuming (and tiring) way to shop, and I don't do it often, but every time I do I turn up at least one gem.

At the top of the range for used clothes are children's consignment stores. The prices here should average about half the retail price in a regular store, but there are advantages to dealing with a consignment store over other options. The way they get their merchandise is through customers like you! Depending on the store, they will either buy your (stain-free, clean, undamaged) outgrown clothes from you outright, or they'll start an account for you and pay you a set percentage of the sales after the fact. In fact, if you've been doing a little smart shopping at yard sales and you're careful about keeping clothes stain free, you may even be able to get back more than you paid to clothe your child originally, and use that money for the next size up! Once Upon a Child is a nationwide franchise consignment store with a pretty good reputation, so they may be a good place for you to start if you have never checked into these stores before. Bonus – they also buy and sell outgrown baby equipment, making them a great place to pick up or sell a swing or stroller! The only things most consignment stores won't deal in are used car seats and cribs, because of the changing safety codes and liability issues.

For those that are still not sold on buying used baby/kid clothing, shop the sale racks and shop off-season. It can be a little tricky buying in the off-season for kids, since you can never be sure just how much they'll grow between this year and next, but the savings can be up to 90% off the ordinary retail price. I've often found that when buying in the off-season, it's better to err on the side of "will be a little big next spring" rather than "should just about fit next spring". If you go a little big, you can turn up cuffs, take in seams, etc. - if you accidentally get "too small", there's very little you can do besides take it to the consignment store or have your own yard sale.

Cribs

A few years ago the regulations on cribs changed – no crib sold (either new or secondhand) can have a drop-side, as they've been deemed too dangerous for use. The new regulations also called for stronger cribs than were made in the past, with heavier slats and more robust supports. The good news is every crib bought new these days will meet the increased standards. The bad news is that it basically crippled the used crib market, and it can be difficult to find a used crib that meets the new standards. In the last few years that started to change, as more of the new cribs made their way to the secondary market, but for now if the crib is more than 6 years old it's not considered "legal".

New cribs are available nearly everywhere – Walmart, Target, Babies' R Us, IKEA, Stork Craft, etc. Remember – if they're being sold new, they comply with the new, sturdier regulations and should hold up just fine. You may be seduced by the gorgeous cherry sleigh crib that turns into a toddler bed and full size headboard, and I agree that they're beautiful. But I have a question – are you going to have any more kids? When baby #2 or #3 comes along, are you planning on spending another $450 - $500 on yet another convertible crib? And the mattress is sold separately! I contend that it's wiser to buy a $100 crib from IKEA (which converts into a toddler daybed anyway), a $40 crib mattress from Walmart, and invest in a real twin bed as they get older.

Oh yes – the crib mattresses. Most doctors agree that all a baby needs is a comfortable, firm surface to sleep on. That can be accomplished with the most basic crib mattresses – I have yet to see a baby that requires a $150 Chiro-guard crib mattress! Just be sure it isn't too soft, as that can lead to smothering if the baby rolls onto their tummy. Same goes for all the beautiful crib bedding – most of it shouldn't even be in a baby's crib, as it can smother a small child. Maryland has actually banned the sale of those thick, quilted bumper pads that seem so popular in the baby décor section of the store, due to the risk of smothering. All that should go in your little one's crib are good crib sheets, MAYBE a ventilated crib bumper (the kind that look like mesh) and warm jammies. No comforters, no plush bumpers, no pillows, no cuddle toys. (That just cut down on your shopping list, didn't it?)

Speaking of IKEA, they have the best prices I've seen on new cribs, high chairs, potties, bibs, feeding gear, baby tubs, simple toys, and baby bedding. Most of these are displayed online, but can only be bought at the store, since they only ship large items. If you're lucky enough to have one within driving distance, I highly recommend a field trip. We have to drive 90 minutes to our nearest IKEA, so we make it a full day trip and have lunch at their cafeteria, and only go about once a year (it's a treat). It's very easy to get overwhelmed and go overboard here, though, so I also recommend making a list with a budget!

One more thing about baby beds – in Finland, every citizen gets a cardboard box filled with baby clothes and other necessities, and the box has a mattress at the bottom to serve as their first bed. I've looked up the dimensions of that box, and it matches the 2 bushel laundry basket available for $9.99 at Target. With a pad at the bottom, you could have a simple, portable bed for your baby. When the baby outgrows the basket, you still have a laundry basket to use, as opposed to a fancy bassinette that is only useful for 2 – 3 months.

Diapers

You knew I had to get to this one sometime. And you're probably remembering the laundry segment, where I mentioned hand-washing cloth diapers for my oldest child and moaning to yourself!

Calm down! Deep breathing (through the mouth, if you're changing a diaper!) will help you.

This book is called Hard Core Poor for a reason, so we're going to start talking about the cheapest option. Cloth diapers. If you're going to do anything to save in your baby's first year, this is it. There are programs that can help you buy formula and food for your baby, subsidies for day care, and charities can help with baby clothing, but please pay attention to what I am about to tell you.

There are NO national programs or funds to help with disposable diapers. WIC and food stamps do NOT cover diapers.

There are a few small, local diaper banks across the country, but generally **you are ON YOUR OWN for diapering your baby.** If you can't afford disposable diapers for a week, your baby's health can suffer with nasty rashes and even skin infections. Children have become gravely ill from skin infections caused by leaving diapers on for far too long, and some have even died. Granted, these were children that might wear the same diaper for 3 days in a row, but I would be doing you a disservice if I didn't make you aware of the risks.

If you are strapped for cash, cloth diapers will allow you to keep your baby clean and healthy, no matter what.

Even if you don't use them full time, at least get a small number of cloth diapers together in case of an emergency, like an unexpected layoff or sudden car repair that used all your cash – consider it a "peace of mind" diaper stash.

Cloth diapers have evolved in the last 20 years – there have even been huge changes in the last 5 years! So let me comfort you first by saying that unless you really want to, you don't need to use a single pin when using modern cloth diapers – they fasten with snaps or Velcro. Plastic pants may still be the cheapest waterproof cover, but they've been outmoded. You don't have to soak dirty diapers in buckets, and if you're changing them often enough, you should not see a leak.

The options available for modern cloth diapers are downright dizzying. If you go online you'll see what looks like alphabet soup – AIO, AI2s, hybrids, pockets, prefolds, contours, covers, wool wraps... and the prices on the fancy diapers can be off-putting too. The best selling cloth diaper on the market, the BumGenius one-size pocket diaper, is $17.95 each. And it's recommended that you have no less than 2 dozen diapers to make sure you have enough between wash loads. Don't worry – Hard Core Poor can tell you how to get enough diapers together for less than $150, and it should see your baby through potty training!

Let's decode those diaper definitions – AIO means "all in one". That means the absorbent cloth and waterproof material are all sewn together, and fastened with either Velcro or plastic snaps. They're the most similar to a disposable diaper, and one of the easiest to put on and take off. Unfortunately, they're also very expensive and they take a loooong time to dry.

AI2s or hybrids are a Velcro or snap on waterproof shell with a snap-in cloth or disposable pad. When the pad is wet, unsnap the dirty/wet pad, toss in your diaper pail or waterproof bag, and snap in a fresh pad. If the shell gets really wet or soiled, you change the whole thing. A little more complicated than an AIO, but more versatile, especially for road trips if you choose to use the disposable pads. The most common brand you'll see of these is gDiapers, and they can be found at Wegmans and Babies' R Us.

Pocket diapers are usually one-size diapers – that means that the size can be adjusted with a few snaps from 8 - 35 lbs, depending on the size and shape of your baby. What makes a pocket diaper a "pocket" is there is an outer waterproof shell, an inner moisture-wicking material like those fancy athletic shirts that wick away sweat, and an opening between the two to stuff with absorbent soaker pads. These diapers are very popular because once they're stuffed with soaker pads, they're as easy as disposables to put on, and when it's time to wash them the absorbent parts come out so they wash and dry more easily. They do use synthetic fabrics which can be a little finicky to wash, but they come with washing instructions from the manufacturer.

The top selling brand (at $17.95 each) is BumGenius, but you can find similar (knock-off) diapers for much less. Kawaii brand diapers are very similar, and cost only $7 each at www.theluvyourbaby.com site. Sunbaby diapers at www.sunbabydiapers.com are also one size pocket diapers, and you can buy a package of 24 with 48 microfiber inserts for $144. (They only sell them in package lots.) Both brands are manufactured in China, however, so if you want to buy American you will pay a premium. (I personally think that buying what you can afford is the American way, but I understand wanting to keep the dollars on our shores.)

Prefolds and covers are a cheaper option, and many people like them even better than the fancier diapers because they're made from cotton, and can be washed and dried with no fuss. Prefold diapers are pretty much what our mothers (or grandmothers) would have used – they're rectangular pieces of fabric that are thicker in the middle, and have to be folded around the baby. The covers are what really make prefolds so much easier to use. The old covers were pull-on plastic pants, and they were a pain when the baby pooped and you had to peel them off carefully. Now covers fasten with snaps or Velcro just like a disposable, and you can simply lay the prefold in the cover and fasten it around your baby. Just like with the hybrid diapers, you can change the diaper but keep the same cover unless it gets really yucky or soiled. The Cotton Babies company makes a seriously good package of prefolds and one-size covers called Econobum. You get 3 one size covers, a dozen really thick prefolds, and a waterproof "wet bag" for $50. Two packages will give you enough to diaper your baby full time, and they're an American company. $100 to diaper your baby – what a deal!

Even cheaper than prefolds are "flats" – a single layer of cotton (flannel, jersey, terrycloth, or gauze) folded to fit a baby of any size. You can find loads of tutorials on how to fold these so they fit and absorb well online. They can be folded and laid into a cover just like a prefold, making them very easy to use. Flats can be hemmed old towels, large 100% cotton t-shirts, receiving blankets, flour sack towels – anything that will absorb well. At first they seem too thin to be absorbent enough, but there's something about the layers and space between the layers when a flat is folded that holds much more than you would expect. The best part about flats is that they wash clean very easily and dry quickly, making them the best diaper choice for a Hard Core Poor mama who has to wash the diapers by hand.

My favorite resource for flat diaper use is www.dirtydiaperlaundry.com – when she heard that some strapped families were rinsing and re-using disposables, she spearheaded the week long Flats and Hand Washing Challenge. As of this writing, the Challenge has happened 4 years in a row with over 200 participants each year, and each year the participants share their experiences and tricks they learned over the week. She has a number of videos showing how you can make flat diapers out of t-shirts, how to hand wash diapers, how to fold flats, and even how to make a very decent, moisture-resistant, no-sew diaper cover out of polar fleece. If you're really strapped, go to her website and do a search on "frugal diaper stash" – you'll come away with ways to cloth diaper your baby full time for less than $20.

We've run down the types of diapers, but now that they've been worn, what do you do, especially with the poop?

If the baby isn't eating solids yet, this won't be so bad – just leave everything alone in the diaper pail, dump in the washer, give it a cold rinse and a hot wash with a little detergent, and two rinses.

For a baby eating solids, you should dump as much of the poop into the toilet as you can. (This is also recommended for disposable diapers. It's right on their package – don't put poop in the trash, put it in the toilet!) You can shake the diaper over the toilet, you can use a designated rubber spatula to scrape into the toilet, you can use a squeeze sport bottle to spray the poop off, you can get a special sprayer to hook up to your toilet supply and spray the diaper, or you can even dunk the diaper into the toilet to get the poop off. After you get off as much poop as you can, put it in the pail and wash just like the breastfed diapers. Cold rinse, Hot wash with a little detergent, two rinses.

As far as detergent, I've found that All Free and Clear, Purex Free, or Tide Free work just fine. I haven't tried the homemade recipe detergent that is in this book on diapers yet, but I'd suggest just using that on the regular clothes and keeping the Free and Clear for the diapers. One of the quirks about washing diapers is that if you use too much detergent (more than line 2 in the detergent cap on a regular basis), it can build up in the diaper like glue and prevent it from getting as clean as it should. This is mostly a problem with pocket diapers and microfiber inserts – cotton prefolds don't have this issue as badly. Just use hot water for the wash, rinse at least twice every time, and about once a month washing with a half a cup of bleach will knock out any germs you have lingering in there. If you end up with build up, take 1 – 2 tablespoons of Dawn dish detergent (blue, original), and wash your diapers with it – then use as many rinse cycles as it takes for the suds to go away – your diapers will be like new!

There are some of you who will cry "But wait! Daycare won't take cloth diapers!", and you raise a good point. Without getting into the mommy wars or ethics of "you should stay home/you should go to work", daycare centers are not the only game in town. There are other ways to make sure your child is safe and cared for. (I also think day care is a germ petri dish – my kids were ALWAYS getting sick there.) You can do this by having one parent at home, working with an accommodating relative or friend who will watch your baby at a bargain rate, or one parent working full time during the day and the other part-time on evenings and weekends so someone is always with the baby. (It's a hard schedule, but it doesn't have to be forever.) If you can swing a schedule like that, the diapers might not be an issue.

However, if you're doing this as a single parent, daycare in some form is a necessity – you have bills to pay, mouths to feed and gas tanks to fill. I know I did. If you find that day care centers are your best option, you still have ways to save money on diapers. First, get the easiest-to-use cloth diapers you can afford, like pocket diapers, and demonstrate HOW easy they are to use.

(They might have awful visions of pins and plastic pants when you say "cloth", so show them what it's really like.) Tell the caregivers that you'll bring clean diapers every morning, take the dirty ones home every night for washing, and all they have to do is put the "used" diapers in the waterproof bag that you leave with them. They might agree!

I've been informed that it is perfectly legal for a day care to use cloth diapers as long as the parent provides enough of them for the whole day, so if they try to say "it's illegal", they're not well informed or making an excuse. Some parents explain that their child will get rashes with disposables, and cloth is for their health, which usually gets their attention and respect. I've even heard from moms that got a note from their pediatrician stating that cloth diapers are ideal for their baby's health.

If after all that they still don't agree, you can still use cloth at home and on the weekends, and save the (generic) disposables for daycare – even part-time use will help you save money.

So cloth diapers are really cheap, but how expensive are disposables? By comparison, for Walmart's store brand disposable diapers a value pack costs $19.77, and contains between 92 and 144 diapers depending on size – the bigger the diaper size, the fewer are in a pack. The Walmart website very kindly calculates the price per diaper as being anywhere from $0.14 to $0.21 each. A baby should be changed on average between 8 and 10 times a day. Using an average of 9 changes, and an average price of $0.17 per diaper, that runs around $45.90 per MONTH in diapers alone. And that's if you use generics! For Pampers Baby Dry diapers, the cost ranges from $0.19 to $0.37 per diaper, with an average cost of $0.25 each. That's $67.50 a month if you don't have coupons, and always buy the large bargain packs.

If you occasionally buy a small pack because you can't afford the big one, you're going to pay more per diaper. I actually saw mini-packs of disposables at Dollar Tree - $1 for 4 - 5 diapers, so 20 to 25 cents per diaper. When you're scraping 2 dollars out of the change cup to diaper your child, 8 - 10 diapers might get you through the day until your paycheck clears, but you don't want to pay that much very often.

The average child will potty train at about 2.5 years old. For 30 months of disposables, you can expect to pay between $1377 and $2916! For a one time outlay of $20 to $400 for a stash of cloth diapers, the difference is pretty stark.

If you still choose to use disposables, or if you want to use them part time for outings or overnight, I suggest sticking with store brand diapers unless they give your baby a rash. Find coupons if possible, and always buy the largest package to get the best price per diaper. (There is an exception to this – sometimes with combining sales and coupons, buying several small packages of diapers will be cheaper than the big pack, but in my experience this is rare for diapers.) If in doubt about which diaper is the best bargain, divide the price on the package by the number of diapers in the box to get the price per diaper. I know, sometimes when things are really tight, you just grab the small box because it costs less, but you'll end up paying more per diaper that way.

Personally, I have a large stash of 7 dozen prefolds (2 dozen small, 2 dozen medium, 2 dozen large, 1 dozen toddler sizes) and about 20 waterproof covers that I got new and secondhand for a total outlay of $250, for my third baby. It's a very basic, boring stash – no fancy prints or styles, just functional diapers. I used disposables for the first week or two, and when traveling, but I was disappointed – they leaked! My cloth never leaked! Besides that, changing a disposable feels like throwing a quarter in the trash, and my baby got a rash from the elastic in the diapers.

OK – all done with diaper talk!

Assorted Baby Gear

Swings, pack-n-plays, exersaucers, bouncy seats, strollers, high chairs, changing tables, etc. can all be bought secondhand. Always check the gear to make sure it's still in good, safe working order, and if possible look the item up online to be sure that there hasn't been a recall on that particular model. If you buy new or used for your first baby and it's a girl, resist the temptation to buy all pink strollers, car seats, swings, etc. It's a trick by the manufacturer to make sure you buy new gear for each child! If you have a second child that's not a girl, very few daddies will feel comfortable with Junior riding in a bubble gum pink stroller, no matter how much you paid for it three years ago. Stick with gender neutral prints that hide stains, and you'll get the best value out of your gear.

Do you need all the widgets that are out there? Of course not! But some really do make life easier – strollers, for example. You don't really NEED a super-fancy top-of-the-line stroller, but if you use a stroller you need something that's comfortable to push, comfortable for baby to ride, and folds easily – there are loads of models like that available used. A jogging stroller is great if you're into running or covering a lot of rough terrain, but in almost every other situation they're just too big and cumbersome. Umbrella strollers fold up tiny, and they're cheap and lightweight, but they're not very good for tiny babies and can be awkward to push. A basic mid-range stroller with large-ish wheels and a good sized carrying basket that folds well is all most parents need. My kids barely rode in a stroller until they were over 6 months old, preferring my arms or a baby sling or carrier. After they got to 6 months, my arms and back were more than happy for the break a stroller could offer!

Another lifesaver (for me and many others) are baby carriers like slings, front packs, and backpacks. Babies love to be held, and these let you keep your baby happy and still have your hands free to get things done! Besides, they're awesome if you're trying to get through a crowd with your little one. A stroller can be hard to get through crowds or tight spaces, but a carrier lets you squeeze through nearly anywhere with your baby. There are loads of styles, and they're ALWAYS available at secondhand shops – try them on, see what you like best. There have been days in our home when dinner would not have been cooked and laundry would not have gotten done without the baby backpack.

As for the other gear, you can get away without a lot of it. Some babies love motorized swings, some seem to see them as a baby torture device. Same goes for bouncy seats. Pack-n-plays are nice for naps at Grandma's house, as a crib in a small home, or travel, but I know a mom of 7 who simply folds a thick blanket as a pad and lays her baby on the floor – she never uses a pack-n-play. As a containment device for crawling/toddling babies, though, they're pretty handy. I never really used my changing table, I just grabbed my changing stuff and laid the baby on the floor, bed, or couch with a changing pad. It really all depends on what suits you and your baby best. The main thing to remember is – don't pay retail! Buy used or borrow from friends, enjoy for a few months, and pass it on.

School

Boy, they grow up fast! Until your child is "school age", it can be pricey to send them to preschool, but if your income is low enough your child may be eligible for Head Start, a free preschool program.

After your child turns 5, the cheapest education available in the U.S. is public school. If you live in a good school district and you're happy with the school system, you have nothing to worry about! In fact, it's so taken for granted that most residents will use the public school system that it's one of the first things parents look at in a real estate listing. In our area, the more desirable school districts lie side by side with failing schools, and it can cause the price of a house or apartment to jump dramatically if it's on the right side of the district line. If you live in an affordable home in a less desirable neighborhood with sketchy schools, or your child has a personality clash with key people in the school, you may need to look at alternatives to public school.

The first alternative most people turn to is private school. Many are religious in nature, though it is possible to find secular private schools in most areas. The tuition for private school varies pretty wildly – in Harrisburg, PA (an area with a relatively low cost of living) there's a small secular private school that charges as much as $11,250 a year to educate your child, though they have a sliding scale that will bring that down to around $3,000 based on income. The Harrisburg Christian School charges between $6,000 and $7,000 a year depending on the grade level of your student. The Catholic schools tend to be in the $3,000 to $5,000 range per year for elementary grades and $5,000 - $9,000 for high school grades, with church members getting a price break. Most schools offer a discount if you have more than one child enrolled, and there are usually income-based scholarships available to help reduce the cost for families who don't have money to burn. Some parents calculate the added cost of moving to a nicer school district and the higher mortgage or rent, and figure that private school is cheaper than moving.

If private school is too expensive or you're just not happy with it, another option is a charter school. A charter school is technically a public school, but it's run independently of the local school district.

Because they're public schools, they are already paid for by your tax dollars (FREE). Some are designed to serve certain groups, like intellectually gifted children, but by law they are open to all. They also come in two flavors – brick-and-mortar or cyber charter schools! A brick-and-mortar charter school isn't all that different from a "standard" public school – they involve physically going to a classroom and taking classes with other students. If you're a single parent or two-parents-working household who needs the supervision that a physical school provides, this is the better option for you. The downsides are there may not be a school near you, or it may be full. Physical charter schools usually hold a lottery to see which students can attend – they're quite popular.

Cyber charter schools are growing in popularity, and chances are that they're available in your state now, if they're not coming soon. A cyber charter school is an online school, with an assigned teacher and classes. The parent is referred to as the "learning coach", and is responsible for making sure the child actually completes the assignments. The neat thing about the charter schools is they provide the student with a computer to use for the year, all the books and materials that they'll use for their classes, and even reimburse the family for the cost of the internet during the school year! If your kid has health problems that might give them trouble in a physical school, if they're happier working one-on-one or independently, or if they have trouble focusing in a classroom setting, this might be the better option for them. The downside with this program is the fact that someone needs to be home to help the student with his/her assignments (at least until you're confident that your kid is old enough to be on their own for several hours daily), so someone may have to give up an income to ensure their child is getting an education. There are single parents and dual income families that make cyber schools work, but it usually involves finding a friend or family member who is willing to be the childs "learning coach" during the day or working shift work so someone is home during "school hours". If there's already a stay-at-home parent in the house, then they just have to ask themselves if they are prepared to help their child stay on task – if you're up for the challenge, it can be a great fit for a lot of families!

Some people feel that cyber charter schools are neat, but that they're too regimented or don't "flex" with their child's interests or abilities the way they would like. In those cases, homeschooling might be a better fit! The regulations on homeschooling vary state-by-state, so it's very important to check your laws to see how to homeschool where you live. Homeschooling is legal in all 50 states and territories. Some states make it easier to comply legally than others, but I can assure you – Pennsylvania is considered one of the "hardest" states to homeschool in, and it's not all that bad. I homeschool one of my children, and I just have to maintain a portfolio of what he's learned for the year, have it evaluated by a qualified person (usually a current or retired teacher), and submit the evaluation to the school district. Really not bad.

But aside from the legal complications, homeschool curriculum can cost a pretty penny! If you choose a "boxed curriculum" that gives you all your subjects and daily assignments, you can expect to pay $400 or more per grade level. That's a bargain compared to private school tuition, but not cheap by any means. If you're a creative, organized person, you can buy used books from Amazon and collect free and cheap unit studies online. In fact, I've scored excellent used math books for a penny plus $3.99 shipping on Amazon. But Hard Core Poor people know how to cut the costs even more! There are several comprehensive curricula online for FREE. And when I say free, I mean the books are online in the public domain, the activities are free, and all you need to buy are printer cartridges, paper, pencils, and crayons.

Ambleside Online is a famous free online curriculum with the goal of replicating Charlotte Mason teaching methods (the focus with Charlotte Mason is on really good books and nature studies). Religious bent is Christian, with heavy Reformation study.

Mater Amibilis is a similar Charlotte Mason curriculum for K – 8, but with Catholic-centered religious teachings.

Easy Peasy All in One Homeschool is a complete K-12 curriculum that lays out all the assignments for the whole year, 180 days, and all the reading passages are hyperlinked, so there's no searching or hunting for the right book online. This mom who developed this curriculum has 6 children, so she tried to make it user-friendly enough that the student(s) could work independently for most of their day. Christian-based in nature, the writer believes in a literal 6 day creation, but the materials used are the standard "old Earth" with a few side notes from the writer about her views.

Discoveryk12.com also offers a free online curriculum, and theirs is secular, for those looking for a non-religious curriculum. It's designed to be accessible from tablets and cell phones as well as standard computers, which makes it easy to use anywhere. You need to sign up with an account, but the accounts are free, and they help you keep track of the students progress.

And as a tax payer in Pennsylvania, if I choose, I am entitled to the loan of any and all books and materials from the public school that my child WOULD be using if he were attending there.

There are a LOT of different philosophies on how to homeschool, and a LOT more resources than this, so please don't think that my little list here is complete – it's just a place to start your research if you are curious about homeschooling.

College

Hang on, I think I need to go lie down for a while. My oldest is 12, and college is starting to be a consideration, complete with knowing how much it costs these days!

First, college isn't a requirement. Lots of people get through their lives perfectly well without a college degree – they work their way up through different companies, they find something they love to do and throw themselves into it with all they have, they start businesses of their own and hire others to work for them. There are still apprenticeship programs available for "the trades" - electricians, plumbers, masons, carpenters – people that make the world go 'round. My own husband went through an electrician apprenticeship program with the electricians union, and has worked in that field for the last 15 years. Not only are many of these apprenticeship programs free, you can get a job working in the field you're training in, earning money while you learn.

Mike Rowe, formerly of "Dirty Jobs" fame, set up a foundation called mikeroweworks.com, and its purpose is to grant 100% scholarships to trade schools. If an apprenticeship program is not for you, but you (or your child) is interested in a mechanical trade or allied health position, it's worth sending in the application.

"But why worry? Student loans are available, and at a low interest rate!" I know many people in my generation were brought up with the notion that student loans are "good debt", and you'll earn enough with the job you get after graduation to pay them off. In fact, because they qualified for low-interest loans that equaled more than the tuition and fees, the financial aid people encouraged them to take the maximum loan so they'd have extra money to live on as a student. Then, after graduation, they found that the job market had tanked. The twentysomething graduate moving back in with mom and dad is so common it's practically a throwaway joke these days. The jobs that will allow a grad to pay off their loans and live independently became hard to find. Meanwhile the loans get put into deferment, so you don't have to pay right away, but the interest is building – you'll have to pay back much more than you borrowed, all while you're trying to get on your feet financially.

Grandparents might grumble about how they worked their way through college, so why can't these kids today? The sad truth is the cost of college has outpaced inflation by a crazy amount. A recent article showed that one credit hour at Michigan State University in 1979 (the year I was born) cost $24.50. Minimum wage that year was $2.90. For a 12 credit semester, the $294 needed for tuition could be earned in a little over 101 working hours – granted, that doesn't include books or room and board, but that's still only 2 ½ weeks of full-time work at minimum wage to pay for half a school year. A student working all summer could pay for the full year of school, books, meal plan, the dorm fee, and still have a little pocket change for pizza. Compared to today, one credit hour at the same college costs $428.75. The current minimum wage is $7.25 an hour. To pay for 12 credit hours for the semester (and remember, a semester is only half a year), the $5145 could be earned in 710 working hours. That's just shy of 18 weeks or 3 ½ months of full time work to pay for half the year. You could work full time through the year, go to school full time, and still barely make ends meet. It's not the best atmosphere for learning, so keeping the costs down is key.

For "standard" college, the best advice I can give (and which I only wish someone had forced me to do in my youth) is to test out of as many courses as you possibly can with CLEP exams. CLEP offers 33 exams in five subject areas, covering material taught in courses that you may generally take in your first two years of college. By passing a CLEP exam, you can earn college credits, bypassing taking the class for that level. A CLEP exam costs $80 for the testing fee, with maybe $30 more for the study guide. If you pass, you've earned 3 credit hours toward your degree rather than having to sit through a semester of that class. If you have to take the class instead, right now the cost per credit hour at our community college is $250 – a three credit course will cost $750, plus the books for another $150, and gas to get there! And remember – that's community college pricing. State colleges charge upwards of $500 per credit hour, and private universities charge enough to make a grown man weep. TAKE THE TEST!

Check with your local community college to see if you can do dual enrollment while still in high school – if you can earn college credit and high school credit at the same time, you'll be ahead of the game. You do need to pay the going rate for the class, but it saves time later on, and money by not waiting for next years' tuition hike. AP (advanced placement) courses are also a boost - they're meant to help you test out of the college classes, and in many cases are MORE challenging that the college courses they're supposed to equal. If you're aiming to get into a prestigious school, AP courses are a gold star on that application. In fact, if your school doesn't offer AP courses, you're homeschooled, or you otherwise don't have the opportunity to take AP classes, EdX (https://www.edx.org/high-school-initiative) is now offering FREE online AP courses! They don't count toward college credit on their own – you still have to take the college-administered test for a $91 fee to get college credit – but they are free classes that are designed to help you test out of the freshman level courses in college. There are far worse ways to spend your free time than by doing an online AP class.

I keep mentioning community college here, and it's for a good reason. Community colleges offer the best bang for your buck in education. If you do your first two years at community college and transfer to a four year school, on average you'll pay less for the first two years of college than you will for one year at the four year school!

Community colleges are often looked down on, because they don't have stringent requirements for their students – anyone can enroll in classes. So they're viewed as the school for people who goofed off in high school, and now have to prove something to the college of their choice. I don't look at it that way – I imagine schools as stores. They offer education in brand name and generic, and you're just buying generic education for the first two years before springing for brand name.

Between dual enrollment and testing out of classes, some students find that they can finish a four year degree in 3 years, sometimes even less. That might sound like rushing a student through, but there are good reasons to take less time in college in favor of early graduation. According to the College Board, the average cost of tuition and fees for the 2013–2014 school year was $30,094 at private colleges, $8,893 for state residents at public colleges, and $22,203 for out-of-state residents attending public universities. That's a lot of money.

Another thing that I think every student should do is apply for scholarships. As many as possible. Some are geared for certain populations (race, ethnicity, gender being factors), some are merit-based for students with excellent grades, some are available to anyone who writes the best essay. The local Kiwanis club or other social groups like the Knights of Columbus might offer a $500 scholarship every year – apply for it! That can help pay for books! There are search engines that can help you identify the best scholarship matches for you – just don't fall for any scams that claim they "guarantee a scholarship or your money back" or "we do the legwork for a small fee". You will never see that money again, and often you don't even get a proper list of scholarships in exchange.

Once you're in your four-year school of choice, there are ways to keep costs down.

- First, unless you're close enough to keep living at home, live on campus. Dorm living and meal plans are cheaper than your own apartment, without the added stress of paying for utilities, groceries, and gas to commute to class. Yes, grab something fresh and yummy from the store now and then, but cafeteria food is food you didn't have to worry about cooking while you're studying. You will never have another time in your life where people are preparing your food and housing is not a concern (unless you become very wealthy) – focus that energy on your studies!

- Second, go online for your books. You can find great deals on used textbooks, usually much better than the school store. Just find the ISBN number and do a search.
- Third – if you can get a student job, like being an RA (resident advisor), you can cut your costs even further. I know a young woman who was an RA in college, and her school gave her a cash stipend and free room and board – a nice chunk of change off her bill! One of our local fire fighting companies offers free room and board to student volunteer firefighters. Some companies also offer tuition reimbursement to part time employees, FedEx and Starbucks among them. It may be only $500 a year or it could be much more, depending on how long you've been with the company and if the degree you're seeking is related to

your current or future job with the company.
- Fourth – If you're a good student with a solid grasp of some subjects, offer tutoring to students in earlier grade levels. You can make very reasonable amounts of money (a good bit more than minimum wage) and help someone at the same time.

Finally, there are a small number of accredited colleges that offer free tuition. Berea College, College of the Ozarks, Curtis Institute of Music, Alice Lloyd College, Webb Institute, and Deep Springs College are all tuition-free or offer a full scholarship to each student. There's always a catch, and in this case the catch is you have to qualify for these schools in different ways. The Curtis Institute of Music requires an audition, for example. They might not be a fit for you, but if you investigate you might find a tuition-free college that's right for you!

Increasing income

If things are tight, saving on your expenses is good, but increasing your available money is good too. But if you're already working full time, or you're a designated stay-at-home parent, or your health won't let you work beyond a certain limit, you need creative ways to bring home extra cash.

First, I have to warn you – there are far more scams than legitimate "work from home" opportunities. The FTC estimates that only one in every 55 of those work-at-home opportunities are legitimate. You should NEVER have to pay for a work from home kit. Home businesses are different, and I'll get into that later, but if you are ever told "Send us $49 now for our proven money making kit so you can start making millions in your spare time!" then throw the info away. Better yet, report them to the Better Business Bureau. According to Forbes magazine, the top 16 work-at-home scams are -

- E-commerce cons (they offer to set up your own web store for a hefty fee)
- the "Nigerian Prince" scam where someone overseas offers to share

their fortune with you if you'll help them transfer it to the States (people fall for it every day)
- 1-900 number scams
- Craigslist scams involving fraudulent checks
- bogus data entry jobs
- check cashing "jobs" where you cash a bad check on your own account
- re-shipping packages (it's usually illegal items)
- envelope stuffing (Machines do thousands of envelopes an hour! This is always fake.)
- pyramid schemes
- assembly work making crafts
- medical billing and coding (a real line of work, but the scam lies in them offering kits and guaranteed work for a fee)
- contract typist jobs (same as above)
- name and address compiling
- rebate processing
- mystery shopping (once again, occasionally real work, but enough offers are scams that it makes the list)
- paying fees for a pre-screened list of "scam free job opportunities!"
- guaranteeing a civil service job, like postal worker, if you buy their kit.

I'm not saying that all of the listed jobs are always scams (well, the Nigerian prince always is...) but if you're told you have to pay a fee for a kit or a list of jobs, don't even bother investigating. Dump them like hot coals and take a look at the list I'm about to show you – I won't even charge you an extra fee!

First, are you more interested in running a small business of your own, or are you just interested in earning money? There are lots of home-based businesses that you can buy into, like Avon, Mary Kay, Discovery Toys, Tupperware, DoTerra, Pampered Chef, Usborne Books, etc. The upshot of these companies is that there is instant name recognition – if someone wants food storage, usually they refer even to old deli containers as "Tupperware". The start-up cost is usually fairly low – Avon has been a $10 - $20 starter fee for a long time, Mary Kay is $75, others vary.

The downside is finding customers on a regular basis that need/want your merchandise. Discovery Toys are wonderful, high quality toys, but how many people buy brand new toys every month? So you have to keep stretching outward to find new customers – a good thing, but it can be challenging to make a profit when a lot of your income goes into advertising. Some people do make a nice living with these home based companies, others find that they simply can't make it turn a profit. If you're curious about how REAL people do with your company, type "former Avon rep" or something similar into your search engine. You'll get a lot of pep talks on how happy and wealthy you'll be from your recruiter – it's worth balancing it with information from the people that aren't as excited anymore.

Another kind of home based business is more based on the needs of your community. The blog 'Budgets are Sexy' calls these "side hustles" (if you're inspired by these ideas, they have a list of about 50 "hustles" at their blog – one may work for you!) If you're a stay-at-home parent and your neighbor is a working parent, maybe you can work out a baby sitting arrangement. I have a small side line where I meet my friends' sons' bus a few days a week and watch him for an hour until his mom gets home from work. She just pays me $5 a day for meeting him, which is pretty cheap compared to other alternatives. My kids get a playmate for an hour, I get a few dollars for gas, and she doesn't have to rush home or cut her hours short because she knows he's in good hands.

I have a friend who makes killer cookies and pies every Christmas, selling them $5 or $6 for a dozen huge cookies and $8 - $10 for a pie. I know a few women who have started very successful house and office cleaning businesses, some of whom bring their children along, some of whom simply work when their spouse is home. More than a few people in this region grow vegetables and fruit, selling their extras on a table outside for a few dollars. Green thumbed people also start their own plants from seeds in the spring, selling the started tomato plants, strawberry runners, and pepper plants for $1 - $2 each. Dog walking is popular, but a growing business is dog poop clean up! Get a few houses on a weekly schedule and you'll have plenty of job security! Back when my brother was young and trying to earn money for a guitar, I heard this tip – go out and get number stencils and reflective spray paint. Go to a neighborhood where the address numbers aren't that easy to see, and offer to paint the number on the curb in front of their house for $5 - $10. If you're not too proud to be seen "trash picking", garbage day can yield lots of treasures to re-sell on craigslist or eBay, and there are some men in my neighborhood that support their families with the money they get from scrap metal recycling.

Maybe all this sounds a little too involved, and you just want to do something on your computer in your down time to earn a little money. You're in luck! There are a lot of sites that offer you money or points in exchange for small tasks or using their search engine. There are actually too many to list, but I'll mention two that I've had success with – Amazon's MTurk program and Swagbucks.

MTurk (short for Mechanical Turk – they explain the name on their site) offers a small amount of money for doing very minor tasks, like Googling a name and reporting how high on the Google page a targeted website popped up. We're mostly talking cents, not dollars, but the tasks are short and the money adds up. This program is through Amazon, so they allow you to add your earnings to your Amazon account as a gift card balance at the $5 level, or if you choose, they'll mail you a check at the $10 level.

Swagbucks.com is formatted differently than MTurk. You can use their search engine, watch TV clips, play games, answer surveys and polls, and they will award you in "Swag Bucks". When you collect enough Swag Bucks, you can trade them in for prizes. They do offer physical prizes, but the most popular by far is the $5 Amazon gift card for 450 Swag Bucks. Most other $5 gift cards cost 500 Swag Bucks, and there are a lot of companies represented. There are gas station gift cards ($25 for 2500 Swag Bucks, $50 for 5000), PayPal gift cards, Visa, Target and Walmart gift cards – you can pay for most of your basic needs with any of these. A tip for earning more Swag Bucks is to recruit friends to join – you get a 10% bonus for any Swag Bucks that your recruits earn for life.

One year my husband was laid off a few months before Christmas. The bills were covered by unemployment, but we had very little for anything extra. He sat down to the computer every evening and did surveys, watched TV, played games, and earned more Swag Bucks than I would have believed possible, padding our Christmas budget with over $100 in Amazon gift cards. I worked the swagbucks site and MTurk to bring in a few extra dollars too, and our

Christmas was memorable and fun without an extra job or added debt.

There are a number of bloggers out there, and some of them make a little money from ad revenue, paid reviews of merchandise, and affiliate links (a small kick back from a company similar to a finders fee, when a customer clicks to the store through the blob link). If you enjoy writing, blog platforms are free and easily monetized. To build a following requires frequent posting, interesting topics (or interesting takes on ordinary topics), and research. I'm Facebook friends with the writer of a very popular frugality blog, Penniless Parenting, and she often posts new material daily, sometimes twice daily. Her articles are interesting and highly visited because she's not afraid to post about weird or controversial things, like cloth "toilet paper". Unfortunately, that also leaves her open to criticism from online trolls, who get their kicks from running other people down. I love when people choose to write, because it's good for the mind and the soul – just be aware that when you put your writing out there, you open yourself to both positive and negative comments. As "Penny" says, you really need a thick skin to be an online writer. One of the best and worst things that can happen is a post you write goes viral – you'll get lots of traffic, good and bad. It could lead to your blog becoming highly successful, or it could lead to you wanting to avoid the internet for a few months.

If you have your own vehicle and don't mind driving, in many areas you can sign up as a driver for Uber or Lyft – both are app based systems that link a person who needs a ride with a driver. You need to be 21 or over with a license, insurance, and your own car, which needs to be at least a year 2000 model or newer in very good shape. The cleaner and nicer your car and service is, the better ratings you'll get on the app. Payment for Lyft and Uber comes directly through their app digitally, so it's cash free. Since there are no anti-competition clauses in the driver agreements, you can actually sign up as a driver for both services if they're in your area. This is a great way to make some extra money if you've recently been laid off and need to earn some quickly, but it requires a lot of flexibility in your schedule and a willingness to work late hours, since drivers report many of their calls coming when the bars close. It's generally frowned upon to pick up riders when your kids are in the car, too, so this is a better option for a single person or for a family with one person who can stay at home and one who can answer the ride call. Uber will provide you with a dedicated smart phone if you don't currently have one, but you need one of your own to work with Lyft, since this is entirely app-based.

A caution – Uber is experiencing some negative press right now about some of their business practices. Do your research before signing up with any company. And if you know or meet people who want to hire a driver, you can always drive them and let them pay you directly – the Uber and Lyft apps just make it easier to get the drivers and riders together.

All of these ideas will bring in some extra money, but it's unlikely that any one of them will pay all your bills. These ideas are more for paying down a loan, keeping the gas tank full, saving for Christmas, etc. than paying a mortgage. If you combined a few ideas, though, you very well could be self-supporting on side-line businesses!

When You're Out of the Woods

You have worked so long and so hard. You followed a budget, used money saving tricks, and paid off your debts. Now what?

That's up to you! And that's the real glory of no longer owing all your money to creditors and having low expenses – you can now CHOOSE what you spend your time and money on. You can save up for something fun, for college, for retirement, or just have a nice emergency fund. You can go on a long-dreamed-of trip. You can buy a NICE car. You're allowed!

I pray that everyone of you who reads this book will someday be able to break free from debt and live the live the life of your dreams. Dream big, dream wide! Dream of the future you can make for yourself and your family without debt, where you will be in a position to help others. And I have no doubt that you will help others when you see the need, because you remember the struggle of your Hard Core Poor days.

And as you do, you'll smile a little. Because you're not Hard Core Poor anymore.

www.ingramcontent.com/pod-product-compliance
Lightning Source LLC
Chambersburg PA
CBHW051802170526
45167CB00005B/1850